Your
Story
Matters

Your
Story
Matters

Sharpen Your Writing Skills,
Find Your Voice,
Tell Your Story

Nikesh Shukla

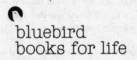
bluebird
books for life

First published 2022 by Bluebird

This paperback edition first published 2023 by Bluebird
an imprint of Pan Macmillan
The Smithson, 6 Briset Street, London EC1M 5NR
EU representative: Macmillan Publishers Ireland Ltd, 1st Floor,
The Liffey Trust Centre, 117–126 Sheriff Street Upper,
Dublin 1, D01 YC43
Associated companies throughout the world
www.panmacmillan.com

ISBN 978-1-5290-5238-1

9 8 7 6 5 4 3 2

A CIP catalogue record for this book is available from the British Library.

Printed and bound by CPI Group (UK) Ltd, Croydon, CR0 4YY

MIX
Paper | Supporting
responsible forestry
FSC
www.fsc.org   FSC® C116313

Visit **www.panmacmillan.com/bluebird** to read more about all our books
and to buy them. You will also find features, author interviews and
news of any author events, and you can sign up for e-newsletters
so that you're always first to hear about our new releases.

*To all the writers I have mentored over the years;
to all the writers I have learned from, laughed with,
performed alongside, read, listened to, enjoyed a silence
with, eaten food with and admired from afar: you taught
me everything I know.*

In memory of Steelo Brown (1977-2022)

Contents

The bottom line is this: You write in order to change the world, knowing perfectly well that you probably can't, but also knowing that literature is indispensable to the world. In some way, your aspirations and concern for a single man in fact do begin to change the world. The world changes according to the way people see it, and if you alter, even by a millimeter, the way a person looks or people look at reality, then you can change it.

JAMES BALDWIN

INTRODUCTION
Whose story matters?

Your story matters.

That's all I have to say on the subject. Your. Story. Matters. That's the message of this book. It's taken me a long time to admit this to myself about my own work, so this will save you decades of self-doubt and imposter syndrome. I'll repeat it again: your story matters.

Now I've set out my stall, let's move to you, what this book is and how it'll help you write the thing you're trying to write.

Actually, no. Hold up. Let's reload this. Wheel it back for a second. Let's say it again, this time as an affirmation. Say it with me. You ready?

My story matters.

Before we do anything else, I want you to grab a bit of paper, maybe an index card, or tear a page out of a notebook. Grab a pen, something that'll make a statement. A bold pen choice. Write: 'MY STORY MATTERS' on it. Sit with that thought for a second. Now stick the paper or card (or whatever you wrote on) up somewhere you will see every day. On your bathroom mirror. In the fridge amongst the cheeses, if you live in the type of household that has more than one cheese at any time and you like them all to sit together like a crew in the cool air of the top shelf.

Above your desk, if you have a desk. If you're a hot-desk kinda writer, take a photo of the paper with your phone, email it to yourself and maybe make it the wallpaper on your laptop.

Use it as a bookmark.

Your story matters. In this book, I will help you write it, edit it, hone it, own it and put it out into the world. There will be advice, new ways of thinking and plenty of exercises. By the end of this book, you will have your story, written, in front of you. I'm a big believer in offering practical help. Because writing is hard. Writing a novel is hard. Writing an essay is hard. Writing this book you're reading right now was hard. Writing is *hard*. I often listen to writers talk about how they hate writing. And I don't think it's because they actually hate writing. I think it's because writing is hard. And it can reduce you to a monosyllabic, inarticulate space-head sometimes. A disconnect happens between the perfect thought in your head and how it gets represented on the page. There is slippage between brain and typing fingers. And if you don't want to come undone by this slippage, you'll need practical help. Super-short lessons and prompts to help you create what you want to create.

I look at storytelling in the following ways:

- have the idea;
- work out your intentions in writing it;
- trust your instincts through the tricky first draft;
- be mindful of structure and technique in subsequent drafts;
- edit, edit, edit, edit.

One of the reasons I want this book to be practical is because storytelling, especially in dark times, is an important act. Storytelling can help us look within and understand ourselves better; it can be an act of generosity towards others, to make us feel less alone; it can help us look for joy and hope; it can help us to understand complex things that are beyond our control. So with all that said, here is my manifesto on why this all matters now:

1. Your story matters.
2. Learning the technical side of writing is essential, but it should never, ever, override your instincts.
3. You know your story . . . you know it better than anyone, but you must also know *why* you want to tell it, why you're the best person to tell it and why you need to tell it *now*.
4. Right now, the only person that matters is you. And you, the reader, are the person that you, the writer, needs to service. The reader-you demands this story. The writer-you has this story to tell. The writer-you should meet the reader-you's demands in the best way you can.
5. Writing is incredibly hard.
6. This book, like every other creative writing book, is one way of doing it. You have to find your own way, your own voice, your own path as a writer.
7. If you don't tell this story, will anyone else? If the answer is 'no', how does that make you feel?

Most writing guides are too focused on making your work publishable, on revealing what will make a publisher sit up and go, 'Send this to the publishing factory immediately; it's perfect, you're the next [insert current cool white writer du jour here].' The vast majority of writing guides are functional in that way. They help you get published; help you write a bestseller; help you morph what you want to do to fit a publisher's vision. I cannot help you get published.

We're going to do things differently.

Writing a bestseller isn't why you're reading this book.

This book is for those of you who want to write, know you have a story to tell, know you have something important to say, and don't know how to start, how to go on, and what to do when you're done.

This book is concerned with one thing and one thing only:

You need to tell your story.

Only you can write the book that you want to write. Only you can tell the story you want to tell, in the way it needs to be told.

My aim is all about taking you back to that original intent. Why you want to write and what you want to write and how you can get the best out of your work.

If *we* don't think our stories are the most important ones out there, why will anyone else?

I remember once talking to a friend about creating work. He put it simply: be the first customer of anything you do.

Besides the obvious, the only equipment you're going to need over the course of this book and its prompts is as follows:

- time;
- thought.

That's it.

There will be lots of opportunities to write, either responding to various prompts I give you, or developing the project you want to work on.

Why do we tell stories?

Why are we compelled to tell stories? This is a question I sit with a lot. What is the function of a story? Of fiction? Of journalism? Of recording a life experience for you in some form? Can writing ever truly teach us empathy? Should it be a mirror, to show ourselves who we are? Should it be a window into the universes of others? What about entertainment? Could it be all these things? None? What expectations should we place on the story? On the storyteller?

Can a screenwriter create a world in a technical schematic (or script)? Can sci-fi offer escape or parallels? What about non-fiction? Can it ever escape the limits of its writer's lens in order to tell us objectively about ourselves? Do blogs change the world?

Why do stories matter?

These are big questions. And if there were an easy answer, believe me, I'd say it here and retire.

I tell stories to make sense of the world as I see it. The world I have lived and experienced, read about and heard about, and what I want it to be. I tell stories to make sense of myself. Most stories tend to wrestle with a question – a big, central, thematic question. Some stories frame those questions as an argument and posit two characters on either side of it. Often those questions can be boiled down to one (or all) of three things: who am I and who could I be? Who should I be?

In a lecture titled 'The I Who Is Not Me', Zadie Smith, author of several critically acclaimed books, from novels and essays to short stories, said that fiction asks: 'what if things were other than they are . . . what if I was different than I am?' Stories here ask us to look within and question not who we are in the present, but also who we have the capacity to be. It's not stretching the truth to say that a good story, a heartfelt story, one that bleeds on the page, a story that isn't written from a position of intellectual superiority, will ask questions about identity.

Stories can explore this central question of identity, using patterns and structures that are familiar, to push characters to see something within themselves that has been untapped for a long time. And through that lens, the important points of the character's journey, we get to understand the world around us, and our place in it – the depths, limits and expanse of the human condition. To quote a terrible Oasis album, we get to understand what it is to be here now.

Patterns and structures, especially in stories, help us find meaning and purpose. Stories help us interrogate and understand the past, the present and the future. Stories give us hope and they cause us pain, both in the writing and in the reading. They entertain us and they challenge us and, through the experience of the narrative, we can contemplate change within ourselves and understand the world better.

I am compelled to tell stories because I don't have a better way of understanding the world and my place in it. I was useless at science and maths. I remember being so frustrated with various teachers for making the answers to these incomprehensible equations seem obvious. The way they taught me maths there was correct and incorrect and no messiness in between. The answer was *obviously* 4.353, or osmosis or stamen. And there was no argument, and I was made to feel stupid for not knowing the answer or understanding how we got there.

Many writers are writers because they have been readers for so long, endlessly chasing the perfect story, before deciding it is high time they write it for themselves. Or they read voraciously – and hate everything they read. Never able to find that perfect balance of character, plot, setting and story that hits all their buttons. The author Chinua Achebe, who wrote the astounding novel *Things Fall Apart*, famously said, 'If you don't like someone's story, write your own.'

I was a shy kid, hanging out in my bedroom most of the time, reading and waiting till I was allowed to watch television. The alternative to television was comics. And when comics weren't available, it was movie tie-in books and *Star Trek* novelizations and *Star Wars* expanded universe novels. They were like TV, except you set the pace in your head. These books were gateway drugs for me. Once I had read all the Han Solo novels stocked in my local library, I moved on to thrillers and sci-fi, hoping to find someone I loved as much as Han Solo. And as I became a teenager, I widened my reading habits in order to find sex scenes in novels to satisfy my raging hormones. Don't judge me. You've done this yourself.

Weirdly, it was being a teenage boy, in the pre-internet era, in search of sex scenes to read or watch that brought me to some of my favourite authors and filmmakers. I discovered Spike Lee, hoping there would be some sex scenes in *Do the Right Thing*. Instead, I was witness to an intense and brilliant story about community, responsibility, race and gentrification. I read *Madame*

Bovary because I read about its sex scenes in a book for teenagers called *The Amazing and Death-Defying Diary of Eugene Dingman* by Paul Zindel. It was the search for sex that brought me to stories. It's funny to think that this, of all things, was what led me to read widely.

My search for sex led me to the book that changed my life and made me realize I had my own voice. That book was *The Buddha of Suburbia* by Hanif Kureishi.

It had loads of sex in it. And it was funny. And it was written by a Brown guy. Which, for the time I found it, and the world in which I sought to come of age, was mind-blowing.

It begins, 'My name is Karim Amir, and I am an Englishman born and bred, almost. I am often considered to be a funny kind of Englishman, a new breed as it were, having emerged from two old histories.'

That 'almost' was the line that got me. The way it rattled around in my head. Helping me understand something I was in the process of figuring out: myself. I remember the day I got that book out of the library. I'd seen trailers for the BBC Two television show – starring a young, beautiful Naveen Andrews, soundtracked by David Bowie – and thought: there's no way my parents are going to let me watch that. It looked like it was filled with sex and drugs and rock and roll and it was definitely not the type of thing I'd want to sit next to my mum and dad and watch in our one-television, mid-nineties household. Also, the timer function on our video recorder was erratic. Also, I would need to start recording the show while Mum and Dad were watching the news and I couldn't risk either of them flicking over to see what I was taping during the local segment.

I needed to watch it, though. I needed to see this outsider Brown kid on this show. All this flashed through my head as I watched the trailer, increasingly despondent that I'd never get to watch this programme. Then came the title card: 'Based on the novel by Hanif Kureishi'.

A-ha. A loophole, I realized. I could get this book out from the library.

My family did not do things together very often. We didn't eat together; we didn't do weekend day trips together; we didn't sit and talk about our days together. My parents worked seven days a week on a small business with my dad's brother, both too tired to do anything other than feed my sister and me, insist that we did our homework, and remind us of our responsibilities: speak good English, study hard and be polite and grateful.

We watched sitcoms together and we went to the library together. My mum and I watched anything with a laughter track growing up. *Desmond's*, *Only Fools and Horses*, *The Real McCoy* to *Red Dwarf*, whatever we could find. There was a comfort in laughing at the tragedies and misfortunes of others. Because, as my mum once put it, 'The only thing separating our lives from a sitcom is a studio audience.' She would joke with me about Dad's business and the various things that would go wrong between two brothers with the best intentions and different styles, who acted like smooth businesspeople but also had to act as everything else in that warehouse, from courier, cleaner and order-packer to HR. She said they were the original Del Boy and Rodney. She'd cast her eyes over to the other side of the room where my father sat in silence with a tumbler of whisky, listening to the sad mournful tones of Rafi, loud enough that we watched everything with the subtitles on.

The lesson I learned from those sitcoms I watched with Mum was that amongst all the pain and hardship, life was inherently funny.

The other thing we did as a family (minus Dad) was go to the library together. There, my library card gave me free rein. I could go wherever I wanted. Nothing was off limits. Mum needed fifteen minutes to find new Mills & Boon books to read and my sister would curl up on a beanbag and stare into space. I could venture into any section I wanted, and pick out any book I wanted.

I'm not saying for a second that every character in a book needs to look like you in order for you to enjoy it. All I'm saying is that at critical times of your life, where you feel like a weirdo, an outsider, someone who doesn't belong, someone alone, be it when you're a kid, a teenager, a young adult or at another transitional time in your life, seeing a version of yourself can be the biggest comfort in the world.

This Brown boy, who felt weird and unattractive and unloved and unliked and different to everyone else around him, needed to see a version of that somewhere somehow.

So at the library, when I saw the name of the author, Hanif Kureishi, I was taken aback. It was a Brown person's name. It felt comforting to me to see a familiar name on the cover of a book. In print. It was tangible. It was real. It could be held. Wasn't Mr Kureishi the name of that guy with the Datsun who drove around north-west London in the eighties, renting out pirated Bollywood VHS tapes to South Asian families from his boot? Kureishi felt like family. I opened the book, scanned the opening lines there and then saw that 'almost' . . . I can remember the feeling as I read that word, wrapping itself around me like the orange shawl my ba used to balance on her shoulders. It made me feel less alone.

It was 1993, and I felt like a funny kind of Englishman. I was increasingly caught between two worlds. At home, I found myself speaking Gujarati less and less. The group of Asian kids I hung around with at school was 'affectionately' referred to as 'the Paki posse' by our white counterparts. I was discovering rap and bhangra and, if I was not working with my parents in their warehouse, the odd daytime rave at weekends. Always overhead was that heavy imperative: work hard and take over the family business.

Kureishi's 'almost' got me. Finally, an acknowledged duality, a nuanced fluidity, a spectrum. I didn't have to be one or the other; I could be in-between. I could be almost.

After *The Buddha of Suburbia*, I diligently scanned the spines of every single volume in the adult section of the library, looking for other South Asian names. That book had changed my life: it said everything I felt, saw things through a lens I recognized, made me feel less like a weirdo.

It also unlocked something in my reading. Though I didn't find another South Asian name for a while, I found myself tearing through *Crime and Punishment, Middlemarch, Brave New World,* Adrian Mole. Instead of movie and TV tie-ins, I was reading more of the world. I was heading through time and space, through country and county. I learned about myself, other people, different cultures, my own culture.

In *White Teeth*, Zadie Smith writes: 'There was England, a gigantic mirror, and there was Irie, without reflection.' Books are mirrors, and I found my reflection in *The Buddha of Suburbia*. It was enough to show me that I belonged. Thanks to a library, I am 'almost', and that is enough for me. And that's why, to me, stories matter. Whether they offer you escape or comfort, whether they expand your view of the world or cement it, a story can change your life.

Why do I tell stories?

Before we get into the hows and whys and equipment lists and introductory topic of thinking about the stories we want to tell, I want to tell you one of my own. It's about how I was scammed as a teenager. In the end, I realized that my story mattered. It deserved better than what happened. It's also about the first-ever time I was published.

This is my origin story, if you will.

When I was a teenager, I wrote terrible poetry. Like, *really bad*. Worse than yours, I bet. A lot of it was about how every little thing reminds me that we're all going to die one day. I wrote collections and collections of these bad poems, thinking one day I would have my moment. I even named one collection, ironically, *The Eternal Optimist*. Haha. HAHAHAHAHA. Get it? Because the poems are so miserable, maybe, actually, in all that misery, there is an optimism. Maybe the world is so screwed that to be an optimist is to recognize how fucked we all are.

HA. HAHAHAHA. Oh dear, thirteen-year-old Kesh. Oh dear.

In 1996, I found an advert for the International Poetry Competition in the back of my local newspaper. I was fifteen years old and ready for my poetry to be unleashed on the world.

I submitted a poem called 'Trail of Thought'. If you ever wrote bad poetry as a teenager, you'll have written something like 'Trail of Thought'. In the poem, I went for a walk and noticed small, poignant things in nature, and each one reminded me that we were all going to die one day.

I filled out the form, printed the poem and sent it off, fingers crossed. I waited to hear back; I carried on writing; I probably finished another collection, who knows? I was prolific at bad poetry.

Then I got a letter. From the International Society of Poetry. I opened the envelope carefully, in case a prize-winning cheque fell out.

I hadn't won.

But they liked my poem enough to include it in their anthology, *Awaken to a Dream*. I closed my eyes. I wanted to scream with happiness. I was going to be a published poet. All I had to do to be published was accept the terms and pay £45 (plus £5 package and posting) for an anthology. If I didn't buy a copy of the anthology, my poem wouldn't be included.

I had to try to convince my mum, who thought my writing a frivolous pastime, to part with £50. She even asked the question – which, at the time, *did not matter* – 'Why do you have to pay to be in this book? Shouldn't they be paying you?'

Nevertheless, my nagging worked and she wrote a cheque for £50 to the Society and I returned it with my letter of agreement. I was about to be a published poet. This is what it had all been leading to.

The months I waited for the anthology were excruciating. I couldn't write anything. It was as if, now I was published, it mattered more what I committed to the page and I didn't want to write anything down unless it was good enough to go into an anthology like *Awaken to a Dream*.

Then the book arrived. The first thing I had ever been

published in. A book called *Awaken to a Dream*, featuring a blistering take on the mundanity of mortality by yours truly. I opened the package to find a book. Containing my work. The first thing that struck me about the book was that it was bigger than A4. And it was thick. Over 700 pages, to be exact. And on each page was a poem, next to another poem, next to another poem. The type was small and the paper itself was almost thin enough to line cake tins with. With four to five poems a page and over 700 pages, I had a sinking realization. This was a scam. If there were thousands of poems and each one cost the author £45 (plus £5 package and posting), the International Society of Poetry was sitting on a fortune.

I was humiliated. Everyone who had submitted something to the International Poetry Competition had fallen for the same scam. I couldn't bring myself to show my mum. And to her credit, she never asked to see it. She must have known it was a scam and if the price of me learning a lesson was £50 we didn't really have, then so be it.

This is why that book is my origin story. Because I resolved to keep writing and to ensure that my precious words found a home worthy of them. Or at least, that's how I justify falling for a scam more than twenty years later. Because your first time being published should be special, and if I don't convince myself that there was a reason for my first published poem being in a scam vanity book, then what good was it in the first place? At the very least, I could write a bad poem about it. And strangely, someone is selling this book on Amazon at the moment. I wonder how many other contributors carried on writing?

But the point stands: my story matters. So does yours.

Who am I?

Now you know who I am, I'd like to get to know you. I'm going to tell you a little about who I think you are, or who I imagine you to be, or who would benefit the most from a book like this.

You, dear reader, are a writer. If you write, you're a writer. You're not an aspiring writer. You don't want to be a writer. You are a writer. You tell stories. You put words on the page and you blur the lines between your reality and mine. You commune with me. Together, we seek to redefine the way people see the world.

I have no expectations of your experience here. My only expectation is that you will turn up and do the work. This is a book to be taken as needed. Dip in as much as you want. Use this book as a comfort blanket, or a guiding, warm and moisturized hand leading you through the darkness.

You don't need any experience. You don't need to have gone on a residency or done one of those fancy, expensive creative writing courses or a masters. You don't need to have been longlisted for a short-story competition. You don't even necessarily need to be working on a book idea. This book is as much about helping you to figure out what you want to say. All you need to be is someone with a compulsion to tell a story and a willingness to show up to the act of telling it.

There are some very technical exercises and thoughts on writing and structure, and these may seem hard. But writing is hard. And that's okay. Because I'm going to be with you the whole way. This isn't about telling you about structure and sending you off into the wilderness. This is about showing you how structure can complement the instincts you already have.

I teach creative writing and I mentor writers and what I notice is that the moment writers who are self-taught start learning about structure, it makes them mistrust the thing that made them show up in the first place: their instincts. We have to trust our storytelling instincts first and foremost. Before anything else. We have to ensure that this is the story we want to tell and the one we're compelled to tell, that we know why we're telling it and why we're committing it to a page right now. Everything else after that, the technique, the structure, the editing, all that is to complement what we already possess.

As I said earlier, this isn't even really a book about making your work publishable. This is about getting you writing and helping you the get the best out of your voice.

All that other stuff: getting published, getting rave reviews, prizes and so on is great – if that's what you're after – but if that's the case, I recommend some other books.

Right now, all you are is someone who wants to tell *this* story. And I will help you do that.

How do I work?

I mentor a lot of writers, and in this book I will be mentoring you. You have to do the work, the writing, the planning, the thinking, the editing, the frustrated deleting. All of that is down to you.

And I will be alongside you as your critical friend in this situation.

How I work with writers is, first we establish what you want to write, and what your intentions are. A lot of this has to do with voice. So, once we've established your intentions in the writing process, we'll spend time on technical things, such as character development and setting and dialogue. Then we'll talk about editing the first draft, which is about bringing a piece of writing out of your head, where it's perfect and ethereal, into something that will engage a reader.

Then we'll talk about developing your skills going forward.

Then you'll go off and write that masterpiece that you want to work on.

Sound good? You ready?

Me too.

PART 1:

HOW DO I FIND MY VOICE?

Growing up as a rap fan made me understand voice. Each rapper I loved was distinct. But it wasn't the sound emanating from their vocal cords or their delivery that I loved. These were constituent parts of something much bigger.

Because of his cadence, content, delivery, flow and viewpoint, I could always tell when André 3000 was rapping. He had the ability to be political, snarky, funny, vulnerable and angry, seemingly simultaneously, in the same verses. His flow was occasionally breathless as one line blended into another without pause. He sometimes stuttered, other times was like water. He loved forced enjambment. Shoving the ends of sentences into the next line and then immediately starting a new thought. He sped up and your heart raced and in the next line he would slow right down, delivering stabbed, punctuated, cursive phrases. He never sounded like anyone other than himself.

I could say this about any of the rappers I admire: Q-Tip, Kendrick, Kano, Little Simz, Dee Double E, Mos Def (Yasiin Bey), Lauryn Hill, Noname. They only ever sound like themselves.

Mos Def rapped once about staying fluid, even in staccato. And I love that. It says everything about voice. Voice is about fluidity. A sense of naturalness. Voice should never be forced. The best rappers know this.

That natural voice takes a lot of work. As a writer, you have only to sound like yourself.

So, I ask you, right before we dive deeper into this: what do you sound like?

I remember my years as a rapper. Between the ages of twenty-one and twenty-eight, I thought I was going to be the best rapper in the world. The end of the story you know, because you're not sitting here reading a creative writing book by the best rapper in the world. And that's okay. I needed to go on that journey to discover my writing voice. What sort of writer I wanted to be – needed to be.

In the late nineties, I discovered a band called Asian Dub Foundation. Marrying political rap with jungle beats, punk guitars and samples from old Hindi, Qawwali and Bengali songs, the sounds they created were the sum of all the musical influences in my head. After I saw them in concert at the University of London student union in the late nineties, I waited for their lead singer to emerge from his dressing room to say hi to fans. As it so happens, at the time, I was working on my first-ever novel. It was called *Darkie* and it recounted the experience of my uncle who, in 1968, after trying to buy a house and facing racial discrimination, became the first person to bring a case of discrimination under the 1968 Race Relations Act. I had discovered my interest in politics, in social issues, in human rights from listening to the band, looking up everything they referenced and studying a human rights module during an ill-fated law degree. Because when you're a teenager, that's all it takes for you to decide the course of your life. Being an avid reader and wanting to find more stories about British Asians, and because post-*Buddha of Suburbia* the well dried for me, I decided to write my own.

My book, *Darkie*, didn't work. It was too rooted in the politics and not enough in character, story and theme yet. I hadn't breathed life into the man, Mukesh, who acted as a cypher for my uncle, yet. All the characters were stand-ins for the grand political points I wanted to make about immigration and racism and, as a result, I couldn't get past the first 10,000 words.

Eventually, what began life in that book ended up published, but we'll get to that. The point is that I sent that 10,000 words to the singer of Asian Dub Foundation because he sounded interested in it. He generously said he enjoyed it, and that was enough for me. He invited me to hang out. I shared some poetry with him. He said it sounded like I needed to speak these poems. I expressed reservations, being the shy nineteen-year-old I was. He taught me how to rap.

We left the cafe where we shared chaat and chai and walked back to his house. He played some drum breaks, I read him my words and he helped me to find a rhythm. That moment changed everything. It restored everything *Awaken to a Dream* had taken from me. The singer took care and interest and gave me space to say what I needed to.

And it was that space that helped me to try different things and settle on the written word as my preferred method of communicating.

This section is about helping you to find your voice. We're going to take it in parts. Because finding your voice is a tricky thing. It's also one of the most important tools a writer has. Because your voice is unique to you. When you've nailed it, it is, anyway. And voice is hard to teach. So much of it comes from within you.

All I can do is point you in some directions, give you exercises to tease out what you want to write about and how, and ask you questions about your intentions.

So, here's what we're going to do. First, we'll work out what you want to say, what stories you want to tell, what stories only you can tell. Then we'll spend some time with how you're going to tell them. Then we'll move on to the actual writing.

What am I trying to say?

What is the story you're telling? What is it *really* about? Sure, it's about a meteor hurtling towards earth and the hero who will stop at nothing to save humanity. But what's it *really* about? There is story and there is plot. These are separate things. The plot is another word for the things that happen on the page: the hero's montage, the hare-brained mission, the twists and turns. The story? That's what it's all really about.

Craig Mazin, creator of the *Chernobyl* mini-series, often talks about this in the context of the film *When Harry Met Sally . . .* and notes how, in the first scene of the movie, you know exactly what the film is about. Harry and Sally meet, get in a car and have an argument about whether men and women can ever just be friends, or does sex always get in the way? This is the narrative of the film. Every single scene advances this narrative. So, what is your story about? What is the journey the characters are going on? The emotional one. The one that makes us care about them.

The way the film interrogates Harry's central question, about whether sex gets in the way of friendship between men and women, is to posit the alternative theory that friendship leads to a deeper love. *When Harry Met Sally . . .* is about the passage of time. What the writer and director are trying to tell us about time is that it is sometimes what two people need in order to fully and completely fall in love with each other. So actually, the sex stuff, that's all surface, that's to do with the beginning throes of a relationship. The deeper thing, true love, takes time and friendship.

Theme, story and plot

With plot, anything can happen. We are in the imagination business, after all. A meteor hurtles towards earth, threatening extinction; a zombie apocalypse brings together people from disparate parts of society who have to learn to work together to survive; a boy and a girl fall in and out of love over three years at a prestigious Dublin college.

As you can see, anything can happen. That's plot. That's the fun bit.

Story is about something deeper. Story is about what it's *really* about. And to further complicate (or complement) this, theme is about the author's worldview, which invariably dictates the progression of the story, the lens through which it is seen.

It's important to break these terms down because our starting point is theme. We can then move on to story. Then we can move on to plot.

Because knowing your worldview – what you want to discuss – will dictate what form this piece of writing takes. Is it a novel, or a short story? Is it even fiction? Is it, in fact, a piece of reportage, an opinion piece? Is it prose at all? Not a poem? Or a screenplay? Or an interpretive dance?

Knowing the themes you're interested in discussing will help you get to the all-important *what happens*.

So, to go through these again:

A **theme** is the main idea or underlying meaning a writer explores in a novel, short story, or other literary work. It might be about good versus evil, or about love or revenge, or courage or a moral question, like what is the difference between a good person who does bad things and a bad person who does good things? Often, a helpful way of thinking about the theme in the piece of writing you want to do is to phrase it as a question. Such as, how should a person be? Or, what does it take for a community to survive unimaginable horror? Or, what lengths can a hero go to to do good in the world without resorting to bad-guy tactics? A theme phrased as a question can act as a **central thematic argument**. Once we know what question we're using character and plot and story to interrogate, we can start thinking about the theme in terms of story.

A **story** is where we use characters, setting, dialogue, plot or a combination of all these elements to discuss our central thematic question. If the question asked is, 'What lengths can a hero go to to do good in the world without resorting to bad-guy tactics?' we might think, okay, we need a hero with a grey area. For example, they are willing to let one person die to save thousands. We now need an antagonist who will challenge that. And we start building from there. But in order for us to discuss theme in a way that feels like we're not being didactic (and this counts whether we're writing a superhero screenplay, a family saga novel or a piece of non-fiction), we need to populate the text with people who are complicated, who are not going to give us easy answers. People who have flaws. People who have a reason for being the way they are, and that thing needs some attention, some interrogating, in order for us to understand them. So, with that superhero who is willing to let one person die to save thousands, maybe they did once let one person die to save thousands, and the world treats them as a hero, but they are haunted by visions of the person they let die. Maybe that person stalks their dreams, reminding them that this is a moral quandary with no easy answers. Story is about the universal experience. It's essentially where we tie theme to something human and tangible.

Plot is, simply put, what happens on the screen or on the page. Story is the glue that sticks all the pieces of plot together. Plot is giving our characters choices to make, forcing them to accept or reject the consequences of those choices, and moving them towards a conclusion. Again, using the superhero plot, knowing that our theme is about a person's moral compass when it comes to superheroism, and the story is about them combatting their guilt at letting someone die in order to be the hero they're meant to be, a plot that complicates the story and theme might see them battle a villain who represents the worst parts of them – a ghoulish mirror image – and they might end up going out with the mum of the person they let die, but without telling the mum their secret identity.

Now we've established what the difference is between story and plot, let's put them into a few very simple examples before moving on to what you want to write, and working on the themes you wish to explore.

So, *The Lord of the Rings* is about a hobbit who has to chuck a ring into a volcano in order to save the world (plot). It's really about a sheltered person being thrown out into the wider world and having to become braver so they can navigate that world (story). That means, when he finally chucks the ring into the volcano, he has become the bravest version of himself (themes: bravery and courage). And we all cheer because this is a satisfying ending.

In Sally Rooney's *Normal People*, Connell and Marianne are exploring what it is to 'be a normal person' given the different environments they've grown up in. Connell and Marianne meet in their small town and begin an on-again, off-again love affair for the next few years that challenges their sense of self, and their sense of their place in the world (plot). Connell learns what it is to love himself, because this is the starting point in loving someone else, and to do that, he must deconstruct his preconceived notions of a person's place in society. Same for Marianne (story). This is a novel about normality and what that even means today, and about first love (theme – two themes! How rich and lucky we are).

In *The Lord of the Rings* there's a lot of plot and thrilling action, but all these hang off Frodo's story. While Middle Earth erupts in war, his is the most important story because, if he doesn't destroy the ring, everything is lost. He is the last, best hope for peace.

Normal People zeroes in on the smaller moments and intimacies of these characters because through these interactions, we see Connell and Marianne's stories. Both books know what they're really about. And both give us compelling, interesting characters to explore their stories. And because the theme, story and plot all play off one another, the writing feels robust and rounded enough to keep the reader interested.

Let's think about theme before we move on to story. What are you interested in reading? What sorts of stories move you? Can you spot patterns in the types of stories you lean towards?

Let's do a little exercise to start with. If you have the physical copies of what I'm about to ask, go get 'em. Also, grab a notebook and some Post-its. I'm not necessarily saying there is a correlation between the types of stories you love to read and the ones you feel compelled to tell, but this exercise will help you to think about your work in terms of what is behind the words.

Go get your ten favourite books, your ten favourite comics, your ten favourite films or your ten favourite video games and put them in front of you. (Or get ten of whatever you have. You may, like me, like the idea of video games more than actually playing them.) Or list them on a piece of notebook paper.

Now go through each one, one by one, and using the definition of theme above, write down on a Post-it note (one per thing) the main theme or themes in each one. Try and limit yourself to one or two words, three at most.

Once you have your Post-it notes, look at them all and try to group them into piles where you see crossover. Spot patterns. If you can't spot patterns, that's okay as well. Wanting to explore many themes is just as valid as having a single focus. Okay, now you know the themes you enjoy absorbing as a reader, viewer or gamer, are these close to what you might want to explore on the page?

Yes?

Okay, move on to the next bit.

No?

Here's something I try that sometimes helps. If you have a voice recorder, either on your phone or otherwise, record yourself. Go for a walk, if you're able to, and talk through the things you want to write about. Talk it out. To yourself. Don't put pressure on yourself to commit to page. Record yourself for as long as you need. The first recording will be a nonsense fart. Again, that's okay. This process takes time. Mostly, because we often start with the meteorite, or the zombie apocalypse or the students falling in and out of love at a prestigious Dublin college. We don't always start with theme. And theme is an important thing to consider.

Keep talking it out until something emerges. And when it does, move to the first of our prompts.

(A little aside with the prompts before we get to this one: do them all where you write most comfortably, but keep all distractions, like phone and internet, to a minimum.)

Writing Prompt: Find the Story
(1 hour)

So, what is your short story or novel really about? What themes are you exploring? What emotional truths? Because once you know this, you can have your characters save the world from a meteor or fall in and out of love for a decade or anything. The events aren't as important as the story. Really think about what the story is.

1. (30 minutes) Think about your favourite novel. Think about the characters. Maybe get it off the shelf to flick through and re-familiarize yourself. For ten minutes, I want you to think about what it's really about. What are the themes it deals with? What is the story at its core? Write this down. And then think about all the points in the novel the themes crop up. Maybe this one chapter where x happens, and the protagonists react in this way, it's because the story is really about the protagonist's x y or z. Write this all down.

Evaluate your favourite book. Break it down. Understand it.

2. (30 minutes) Do exactly the same thing with the project you're working on. It may be a short story, or a novel or a screenplay. Each of these requires you to know what the story is. So do the work as above. Understand exactly what your story is. When you're finished, tear the paper out of your notebook or print out the document. Stick it up somewhere you will see it. Remind yourself of the story. This is your guide for what you're working on.

Why am I trying to say *this*?

Setting our intentions is important. We need to know why we are telling the stories we want to tell, or even need to tell.

Now you know what your story is really about, at least thematically. So, the next step is to sort out your intentions: why you want to say what you want to say in the first place. It's helpful to create something a bit like a mission statement.

So, remember those four core questions I set out in the Introduction:

1. Why this?
2. Why me?
3. Why now?
4. Who for?

You need to know the answers to all these questions. The answers will get you through the hard times, the slow times, the 'I can't make this goddamn scene work' times and the inevitable rejection times. All approaches are valid. There are no right or wrong answers here. But knowing the answers to these questions will help you. More on rejections in a bit.

So . . . let's break this down:

1. **Why this?** This could have been a poem, a tweet, a conversation, a film, a stray thought, a journal entry, an Instagram caption, a novel, a screenplay, a short story. Why this? Why *this* story? And why tell it in the form you have chosen? What are your reasons for choosing to write a personal essay or narrative non-fiction? Or what is it about this story that requires a novel-length interrogation? Why do these characters need 300 pages of obstacles? Why? Why does this story demand you tell it? Write down why you're choosing the form you're choosing. Why a novel? Why not another form? Why a short story? Why a screenplay? What is it about that form that suits these characters and this story? Write it down now in your notebook. Be sure of why this is the story you have to tell and why this way is your way of telling it. Why this? Why this way?

2. **Why me?** Why do *you* need to write this? If you don't write it, will anyone else? Will it stretch you? Will it stretch culture? Literature? THE WORLD? Do you bring a particular expertise or worldview? Is this something that happened to you? Is this something happening in the world right now and your unique take hasn't been explored yet? What is it about your viewpoint that we need? So . . . ask yourself. Why you? Write this down now, too. The trick here is to not grandstand. Sometimes a story needs to be told because if you don't do it now, you won't ever do it, and the story won't then exist. And that would make you sad. You need it to exist. Sometimes a story needs to be told because you needed to find that story at a particular time of your life and this is your opportunity to rectify the past absence by ensuring no one else feels that absence as well. Sometimes a story needs to exist because no one else will

write it and that doesn't mean it doesn't need to be told. Sometimes a story exists because you need to write it out of your system. Sometimes you write this story because others can't – they don't have the tools, the time or the presence of mind to do it. Sometimes you bear witness.

There are so many untold stories. And we have to tell them. I'm reminded of a quote from Arundhati Roy: 'There's really no such thing as the "voiceless." There are only the deliberately silenced, or the preferably unheard.' So write.

3. **Why now?** Some stories require distance. Some stories require closeness. Hindsight and reflection can radically alter stories. Being in the moment of the story, still living in it, in its consequences, its fallout, can affect a story. So, what is it about now that is compelling you to tell it? Is it to do with the world? You? So why now? You know what I'm going to tell you, right? Write. That. Down. NOW. Why now? Is there a conversation happening that your perspective can add to? Is the simple answer, 'It's now or never'?

4. **Who for?** Stories need readers. Who is the reader? Define them. Tease out what you know about them. This isn't for the faceless masses. This is for someone specific. Identify your reader, write about who they are, why they need this book and what you hope they will get from it. Sometimes the reader is you, and that is more than enough of a reason to do this.

Answer these questions, and what the story is really about, and you have got yourself one hell of a project, my friend.

Writing Prompt: Secret Santa
(60 minutes)

I challenge you to write a short story, max 1,000 words, with the following prompt:

You're at your office Christmas party. You unwrap your secret Santa present. It's a bloodied glove, with a note that says: 'You're next'.

What we want in this story is for you to trust your instinct and let the story take you where you need it to. Don't over-plan. Luxuriate in the wild premise and where that can take you. One thing I can't give you is your own instinct, but I can help you to trust it. And that will bolster your thinking on why you want to tell certain stories and why you *must* tell them now and why you're the best person, the only person, to tell them.

What is the importance of what I'm trying to say? Or, why even bother? A personal response

I often think of story as archive. Buried in countless books is the specificity of a people, a place, a community. And that specificity is rooted in the author's gaze. From sci-fi to fantasy; crime to literary fiction; poetry; and on and on, each one will mirror the world in which we live; tell stories that cannot be forgotten.

My first novel, I wrote about a place at a particular time. I spoke specifically about the place I grew up in as a teenager. I recorded its people, and its social structure and its feel. It was important to document these things because if I didn't, who would?

Kerry Hudson, activist and author of the exceptional books *Lowborn* and *Tony Hogan Bought Me an Ice-Cream Float Before He Stole My Ma*, once said, in a provocation for the National Centre for Writing: 'We are losing stories in the UK. We are narrowing our literary culture. We have a publishing industry which continues to perpetuate its failure to reflect the extraordinary spectrum of communities in this country and so we are losing that potential vitality, social exploration and innovation in the books we publish.'

I don't want us to lose any more stories.

A story captures a reader's imagination because it taps into something universal to the human experience.

A story only keeps a reader going if the specificity of its world is immersive. Sometimes you can read books that feel like tour guides to new places. They will stop and give you the Wikipedia breakdown of that war or this time. Or they will go to great lengths explaining to you how this world works, what powers people wield and what societal structures look like. But the stories that work are the ones that seamlessly reveal the specific and the universal. On the surface, Sally Rooney's *Normal People* is an expert exploration of first love. However, dig deeper and you have a book about class and societal expectations, as Connell and Marianne strive to be what their lot in life dictates as normal. And how does that give them space to come together? Its specificity about Trinity College Dublin and the small town both are from never takes away from the universality of their deep bond, and love for each other. Same with *A Christmas Carol*. Is this a story about a bitter man learning empathy or a comment on the dangers of having more money than you know what to do with? Is money evil?

Of course, if you're a writer from a marginalized background, that specificity can sometimes be your undoing when it comes to how it's viewed by the publishing industry. But I don't want you to lose faith. Before my first novel was published, most publishers told me there wasn't a market for the book and that it was too niche. One told me that the characters didn't feel authentically Asian. Another said that they were already publishing an Indian author that year. Another said there was no plot reason for the characters to be Brown. And yet it didn't deter me from writing the book I wanted to write. Because that specificity of place and culture is what made the book real.

I have never hung out in the West Country of the eighteenth century with posh white people. I have never swung through the skyline of Manhattan with a mask on my face and the fresh sting of a radioactive spider bite on my hand. I have never been to Middlemarch. And without googling, I couldn't confirm whether it's a fictional place or not.

The point is specificity isn't a barrier to readers. Readers enjoy specificity. Whether it's one they recognize or not, readers love immersing themselves into a richly textured world where they feel so convinced of it that they can't see the joins of story woven through the text. Once they're in the story, they will give themselves over to whatever part of the human experience you're trying to reveal.

I don't believe that we need to always see ourselves in stories. But I also don't believe that a story's specificity can put readers off.

When we think about why we tell stories and why it's important to tell them, I think a lot about those writers who were discouraged by their interactions with creative industries, unwilling to see both the specificity and the universality in their stories. Understandably, these writers stopped. We lost those stories. And we cannot afford to lose more stories, as Kerry said. We cannot allow ourselves to become a monocultural space where only one type of story is told, and established writers feel that it is their right and theirs only to hold this space.

Now we move on to another question. What will it mean to you if you tell this story? What will it mean to you if you do not?

We often talk about stakes. In screenplays, we ask ourselves what are the stakes for the characters. What will happen if they do not get what they want or need? What will happen if they do? We don't ask this question enough of writers themselves. What is the personal cost for you of not writing this story?

I sometimes think of the personal cost for me of not writing my second novel, a satire about social media, men and hidden identities. At the time, I was very much in the world of social media. I lived and breathed Twitter. Every thought I had was for it, every event I experienced, I needed to narrate on Twitter. And there were times where I would stretch or embellish the truth and people online who knew me offline would treat me as if this new reality I had described was gospel. People who only knew me online had a specific idea of who they thought I was. And so, writing the book had a huge personal gain for me. I got to track my relationship with social media and the potential dangers of it. If I hadn't written that book, would I have realized that I needed to tweet responsibly?

So far, you've thought about why you're the best person to tell this story. Now let's think about why you need to get it out of your system. Before we do this, I'm going to get you to warm up and put yourself in a creative mode. Dig deep, rather than answer the question straight off the bat in a way that feels reactive.

Because if we were having a coffee right now and I asked you, what would it mean to you to write this story and what would it mean to you to not . . . your brain would probably go blank. In that way that we freeze when someone demands we tell them our ten favourite movies. In the panic of freezing, it often feels like I've never seen a movie before in my life. So, let's head to this little prompt I like to do that takes us on a journey. In a weird way, it's a journey that takes us from one world into the next. From this world here, right now, into the world of creativity. The imagination business, as I like to call it. The world where anything is possible and writing is surmountable and stories are ways of understanding our lives.

Writing Prompt: Warm Up
(15 minutes)

You would never just go to a gym and pick up some weights and start benching a million kgs or whatever. You'd warm up, a gentle loosening run or row, some stretching, something to get the heart rate up before beginning. So here is the writing version of that.

Find something to write on and with. It doesn't matter if it's a laptop or a notebook or a voice memo on a phone. Whatever feels most comfortable.

This is a freewriting exercise, and this is how you will do it.

Set a clock for three minutes. You have three minutes per prompt for five writing prompts. I want you to write what comes out. Don't worry about the sentences. Don't worry about it making sense. A word soup is fine. If one prompt is a poem, another a short story, another a play, that's fine. Find what works for you. You have to keep writing for the full fifteen minutes.

When the three-minute timer goes off, move to the next prompt and reset the timer. Keep going until you have worked through all five prompts. No editing. No second-guessing. No worrying.

Here are your prompts:

A departure
A fork in the road
An old friend resurfaces

A debt is paid
A route home

Ready? GO! See you in fifteen minutes!

[Fifteen minutes later . . .]

You all done? Right, now we are going to put that work to one side. Maybe there is something in it to come back to, but first we need to think about this story of yours and why you want to tell it.

On a fresh bit of paper, electronic or other, I want you to write the answers to these questions:

Why me? (Feel free to repeat what you wrote before; it's okay, intentions must be repeated until they are ingrained.)
What is the cost of me writing this?
What is the cost of me not writing this?
What will I gain by writing this?
What will I lose if I do not?

Go.

How do I work out what I want to achieve?

Okay, so if you're still working out what you want to do and want this book to help you try lots of different things before you commit to a project, be it an essay, a book-length thing or other, this chapter might be one to come back to later on down the line.

Having said that, it might help you with visualizing what you want to get out of writing and telling stories. If your ultimate goal is to try your hand at writing because it's something you've felt you want to do more of, that is totally okay. Goals don't have to be lofty. Or specific. If you're coming to this because you want to write a Booker Prize-winning bestseller, I have to manage your expectations. This isn't the book for that. This is the book for helping you to set your intentions, to understand that what you're doing carries significance and to support you through the process of working.

So read on with this bit and see if it can help you establish what you want to get out of the act of writing. This is an exercise I learned from an excellent life coach, Jo Hunter, that I adapted to help the writers I was working with.

So, if I were mentoring you, this would pretty much be our first session: work out what you want to achieve.

Excuse the crap pun, but growing as a writer involves an acronym: GROW. It's a bit 'manager in office does your professional development plan with you', but it's also a great way to visualize big projects that may feel unwieldy. And it's the best start for those of you who have goals you wish to achieve.

GROW IS: (G)OAL, (R)EALITY, (O)PTIONS, (W)ILL.

So, let's explore these before we get down to the nitty and the gritty of the writing.

GOAL: What do you want to write? Is it something specific or something that is more exploratory? If it's something specific, what do you visualize having at the end of the process? If you don't have anything specific you wish to achieve, then what do you hope to develop, either within yourself or outside yourself and on the page at the end? (You can say, 'I don't know . . . yet,' to this question.) Do you know what you want? What is the goal of the piece of writing? What would a successful, completed piece of work look like? What are the things that are sacred about the story you want to tell? What is sacred about the characters and the plot and the story and the setting and the voice? Most importantly: what is making you want to show up to the page?

REALITY: What is happening right now? Check in on what's happening to you now. What is stopping you? What is holding you back? How important is achieving the writing of this piece to you? Here, you may think about factors that affect how much time you have to give. This may be anything from work, to money, to time, to family, to following a sport and remembering all the names on every team, to anything. I'm not saying you should replace any of these with writing. Be realistic that these all reduce what time you do have to do stuff.

OPTIONS: What could you do to carve out space in your daily life for writing? What would you like this to look like? What are the various options, considering the above realities you've identified? If you had no boundaries? If you had boundaries. Push yourself here. Break your options down into granular items as far as possible. Don't just write 'apply for funding'. List all the organizations offering funding for a writer in your position, all the streams you're eligible for. Don't say you're going to write five days a week, especially if you play a sport on Wednesday evenings and have book club on Thursdays and the weekends get taken up with ferrying children around various clubs and activities and family houses and parties. What are the days, or even, what is the one day a week you can commit to? A day's worth of work is sometimes better than lots of here-and-theres. Keep asking yourself what else and what else and what else and what else.

WILL: Here is the important one. What are you willing to do? What will you do? Be specific; think through every step; make it small and achievable. Make it succinct and time-specific. Check in on your commitment here. What are the realities that are likely to trip you up, and what are the strategies you can employ to overcome them?

It may sound simple: establish your goal, work out what your life looks like, give yourself some options, work out which of those you want to commit to.

A lot of the above is based on a heap of assumptions, like you knowing what you want to do, how you want to do it. That you have to identify all the options in order to decide what is the best route for you. That you know the best way you work. That you have the time, the money, the support. That's why it may not be the best chapter for you right now. It is an important part of the process, though. It can be the difference between writing aimlessly and writing with purpose.

But you know what? Sometimes writing without aim or

consequence can be the thing that makes you fall in love with it enough to develop.

Embarking on a journey of writing the story that lies deep within you is a long, long process. Getting it right is a long, long process. Along the way you will think you're the best writer since Sliced Bread, winner of the [insert prize name here] in 1523, and along the way you will think you're the worst writer since Burnt Toast, loser of every single [insert prize name here] ever awarded. Life will get in the way. Your over-confidence or your lack of confidence will get in the way. A book that someone suggests you read when you soft-pitch them your work as you make small talk at a wedding will make you think, oh no, this is exactly what I want to do, but better. Or even worse, this is exactly what I want to do, but worse, and it's been published, so my superior idea will be filed under 'already done'. Some days you'll think, what *is* the fucking point? You may spend your time writing thinking, I'm enjoying this, but a book idea isn't emerging. Am I wasting my time? A piece of feedback from a loved one (never a good idea to seek out their advice . . . their job is to tell you they love you, and make you cups of your favourite hot comfort drink, not give structural notes on plotting and character arcs) will make you think, this definitely is a waste of time, we could be at the pub right now with our friends talking about a Netflix show or a football match (or something else that doesn't matter as much as this story you need to tell).

You will stumble as you encounter all of these things at some point during the writing process, sometimes simultaneously, sometimes tag-teaming them as a sort of cruel wrestling crew. The GROW model will be your anchor throughout the hard times, and it'll be the reminder of intention through the brief, fleeting periods of your pulsating ego bellowing 'I'm a golden god'.

Writing is hard, and even harder is remembering to keep returning to these exercises with the best intention. You know this work better than anyone. Only you can do what you can do.

This GROW model can be project-changing.

Growing is about getting more comfortable being you on the page and about being able to sound only like yourself. Growth takes time. And confidence fluctuates. Rather than being confident in your talent as a writer, learn to trust that you know what you want to say and do best in your story. Sure, the execution may sometimes need work, the text may need constant refining and the audience may read things into your intention that you didn't intend. But all these things are controllable.

I remember a writer giving me advice about teaching creative writing. We were talking about workshopping work in groups of people. How vulnerable you can feel when your work is torn apart, your sentences rewritten, your characters accused of being cyphers, your plot construed as contrived. She said that the writers that trust themselves the most are the ones who can sit and listen to fifteen people's opinions and make notes and say mm-hmm, and take all the feedback, sit with it, sift through it and work out what's useful and what's not.

'Most writers,' she confessed, 'when they're being workshopped, they want to chip in and tell you, no, it's meant to be that way; no, but later this happens; yeah, I know; no I did it this way because . . .'

Growth is about trusting yourself, and trusting yourself is about knowing what you want to achieve, what the reality is, what you could do to achieve it and what you will do.

Everything else – the writing, the rewriting, the editing, the rewriting, the thinking, the rewriting – feels achievable if you know to trust yourself.

How do I write about tricky subjects, especially ones that cause pain?

I think now is the time to talk about writing our pain, our trauma, our sadness, because often one of the reasons we show up to write is to record or work through these things, to find some closure, catharsis or meaning. And if you're a writer who is showing up for this reason, I think it's important that we address early on that you're going to be drawing on tricky stuff. Especially if you are using your own life as source material.

Whether we intend to or not, we do draw from our own lives when we write, be it people, emotional truths or situations. So, we need to think about how we protect ourselves and how we retain the truth of the experience without necessarily giving readers a blow-by-blow account of the events as they unfolded.

We're not writing to settle scores.

The other thing to consider is that sometimes writing about horrific past traumas doesn't exactly make us leap towards the empty page with enthusiasm. Writing can then be filed as the very last thing we want to do.

So how do we write about sad stuff that makes us too sad to actually write, and write it well?

To help you with that, let me tell you my truth first. And I'm going to be completely honest here. I know that ideally, I should be starting this book as an expert who is going to hold your hand. And much as I know my stuff and I've taught people who've gone on to big things, I'm also a writer, who feels not amazing a lot of the time. The point of telling you what I'm about to tell you isn't to make you lose confidence in me. I'm telling you so you trust me. The only way I can do that, in these early pages, is through being transparent with you about the realities of writing.

Today I didn't want to write. I'm working on a novel that I completed and then threw in the proverbial bin. I started the novel in the wrong way, and forgot it was about people in difficult circumstances, and not a political point I wish to score.

It's so depressing to know that 80,000 unusable words of this novel have been consigned to the scrap heap. It's so depressing to know that the pain and hardship it took to write those 80,000 words feels like it was in vain. It wasn't. It was part of the process. But today I do not feel pragmatic. Today I feel defeated, deflated, and my friend has given me a long-term loan of his old console because he bought a new one. I just want to play the Spider-Man game he has sent with it and swing through the streets of Manhattan carefree.

Is this part of the process? This inertia I feel? The document is open. The cursor is blinking. The dialogue I wrote yesterday is staid and not sounding like anything an actual person would say. If I close the computer, I am defeated. If I write myself into more trouble, I am defeated. If I do something else, I am defeated.

I used to think that showing up was about writing, in the same way that I thought 1,000 words a day was better than 250 good words a day.

How do I write through the sadness? Especially when I don't

have to write? I could do literally anything else. It would be okay if I didn't. The world wouldn't end. The universe wouldn't implode. The engraver wouldn't throw my Booker Prize trophy in the bin and start again.

Stories are our way of asking questions of the world. And the world has felt like a funny place these past few years. Things have felt more uncertain than ever. We feel destabilized. Not only that, but the stuff we want to commit to the page is something we're still processing.

If you feel writing is a comfort and fiction is a way of escaping, of creating for yourself, of imposing purpose on your day, do please keep going. If you feel like you're on a roll and the space you've been gifted is snowballing into words on the page, page after page, keep going.

If the very thought of writing is crushing you down, because how can you escape when everything in the news feels so real, keep going. Keep going with whatever you need to.

Before I tell you how to write through tricky subjects, I need to take a second to reaffirm something with you. It's something I've already said and will continue to say throughout the book. It's not to scare you off. If anything, it's to commiserate and offer solidarity. It needs to be said so your expectations of the process of showing up are managed. And I know this isn't going to scare you off, because you have me and you have this book and you have that story that demands you tell it. But let's say it:

Writing is hard.

It's meant to be hard. If it's too easy to write down the tricky stuff, chances are, you're not digging deep enough. Because here's the truth about writing through the tricky stuff: tell the truth. Tell the emotional truth.

There is the actual, physical, tangible truth of what happened; there is your perspective, and there is the emotional truth in your heart. Knowing what the emotional truth you want to tell is frees you from having to tell it exactly as it happened, or having to constantly mitigate your own perspective with balance, offering perspectives that tell a different emotional truth.

If you stick to the truth, the process will still be hard, but you will be doing yourself a service. Now, I'll drill into techniques later about how to do this in practical terms, and also about narrative perspective and the lens through which we view all the action. In the meantime, you know that this is going to be hard but your best weapon is the truth you wish to wield.

How do I find my voice, then?

Right now, you may have identified things you want to write about, stories you want to tell, or you might still be experimenting with things like style and the type of story you might want to tell. I'm going to get you to try a bunch of different things here just to see what type of writing fits you best. Prompt A is for those of you who know what you want to write about, and prompt B is for those of you who are still working it out.

In terms of the question that opens this section – how do I find my voice, then? – this is a lifelong journey for most writers, myself included. We'll ask ourselves this question again at the end and see if we're closer to where we want to be. Also, remember to keep asking yourself this question. Because as your voice and output grows, what you might want to say will evolve.

Writing Prompt A

Take your theme and write it down at the top of a fresh piece of paper. Look at it. Now, in a later chapter, you're going to try different exercises and styles to home in on the type of writing you feel most comfortable with. Each exercise requires you to write 1,000 words then edit for a day. There are three exercises over seven days. However, because this is day one, we're going to plan what we're doing.

DAY 1: IDEAS

Spend an hour writing down everything you can that's associated with your theme. It could be esoteric, it could be a film or a book that inspired you, it could be facts, it could be sketches of character, it could be a story in your family, it could be an article you read, it could be why this interests you.

So, if you write down love, for example, you might write down the following things:

- *When Harry Met Sally* . . .
- *First Love* by Gwendoline Riley.
- That chaotic *Guardian* blind-date column where they ended up at an orgy.
- My relationship with Raheem/Sara.
- That story Sanjay told me about how he proposed to Gita.
- Love is all-consuming.
- Obsession.

- Those first few months of intense love, where they eclipse everything, versus those last few months, where they are Pluto and you're debating whether they're even a planet.

I could happily keep going, but you get the picture. This is idea generation, teasing out something from an all-encompassing theme into something tangible. Be specific. Think of moments you've experienced, be they a fleeting second where your heart skipped a beat or an evening where you felt so in love you thought you might die (if your theme is love, lol).

Do this for an hour, then take the rest of the day off.

DAY 2: THE SHORT STORY

Here is where you create a protagonist, the person who is exploring something within that theme. It may be about obsessive love. It may be about the first and last day of Raheem's relationship with Sara. It may parallel the two days and how similarly or differently they move. For example, they meet at Suhaimah's birthday and they break up at Suhaimah's birthday the following year. Whatever it is you choose, write a short story, minimum 1,000 words, give it a beginning, middle and end, give yourself a theme to explore, a protagonist who has a big question to ask and an antagonist who questions the question or the worldview of the protagonist. Drive us towards an inevitable ending for those characters.

Give yourself a few hours to do this. Don't worry about making it perfect. This is very much the first draft and I don't want you to linger in those sentences worrying about making them perfect. Not yet.

DAY 3: EDIT

Read through your work from yesterday. How does it feel? Does it feel like something you enjoyed? Did you like living in fiction, building a world and choosing two characters to exist within it? Spend an hour or two editing this short story and rewriting where necessary. Get it to a standard you're okay with.

DAY 4: THE PERSONAL ESSAY

I want you to write a 1,000-word personal essay exploring the theme you have chosen.

Pick a moment from your own life and use it to respond to the world at large. For example, if we're continuing on the theme of love that I've chosen, I might, for example, write about what I know of how my parents met and what that teaches me about first love. I might recreate the Diwali function in Huddersfield where my dad went from London to watch, visiting his cousin, who happened to be married to my mum's eldest brother. I might write about the moment he saw my mum, onstage, doing a dance, and how he had that Carpenters moment of birds appearing, suddenly.

I might write about how that affected my perception of love, of romantic love, how it was so filmic, almost rom-com-y, that it led me to obsess over how I might meet the love of my life and have those birds appear. I might do deep dives into meet-cutes in romcoms I obsessed over, thinking they mirrored my parents' own story, and finally ending with how I met the love of my life at a conference for paediatric doctors in an anonymous conference hall while I was flyering for a gig I was doing, that would turn out to be terrible, and across the conference hall chairs and foldable tables and flyers about services and products for paediatric nurses, I might see a girl and those birds might suddenly appear.

What is your personal connection to this theme? That's what we're trying to work out. And how it feeds into a wider story. What is the big question that one tiny, significant moment can act as a catalyst for? What can we learn about the world from your story? It can be big or small. It has to be relatable. How does it refigure or clarify how you see things?

Get that done in 1,000 words and take the rest of the day off. See you tomorrow.

DAY 5: EDIT

It's edit day again, so read through your work from yesterday. How does it feel? Does it feel like something you enjoyed? Did you like using your life, your opinions, your worldview as a way of exploring a theme? Did you find this an easy task? How much did you find yourself struggling? How much did you put on the page? What's missing? Spend an hour or two editing this personal essay and rewriting where necessary. Get it to a standard you're okay with.

DAY 6: THE POEM

Time to write a poem. Now I can't give you much instruction on the form and texture of a poem. That's not my speciality. I'd recommend seeking out Anthony Anaxagorou's book *How to Write*, which is great on this. What I would say is, I want you to distil your theme into a single image, metaphor or moment. The thing with poetry is that you can be personal without ever appearing on the page. You can use language in a way that is freer than prose when it comes to storytelling. This may be a good way for you to think about your voice. Writing is a series of conversations we are having with each other and with the world, and the way a poem can realign our vision, our thematic concerns, our approach to telling a story, can be empowering. So take the theme and conjure up an image. A single image, metaphor, moment. And write. Don't worry about rhyming, form, stanza, anything. Be natural. This is a freewrite. Let the words arrive on the page. And if you're stuck, put whatever comes into your head down. All approaches are valid. Take as long as you need.

DAY 7: EDIT

It's edit day, so go through your piece with fresh eyes. Does it explore thematically what you wanted to? Do you think it would be clear to a reader who doesn't know you? How does it feel? Does it feel like something you enjoyed?

After this week, decide which piece you would like to develop and get it to a standard you're happy with. Attempting different types of writing will point you in the direction of what works for you.

Writing Prompt B

For those who are less certain about what you want to write and how you want to write it, here is your week of prompts.

DAY 1: THE SHORT STORY

Your prompt is this opening line: 'The day she walked into that cafe, she knew everything was going to be different.'

Take this as your first sentence and write a short story, a minimum of 1,000 words. Give it a beginning, middle and end, give yourself a theme to explore. Add a protagonist who has a big question to ask and an antagonist who questions the worldview of the protagonist. Drive us towards an inevitable ending for those characters.

Give yourself a few hours for this. Don't worry about making it perfect. This is very much a first draft, so don't linger on sentences trying to make them perfect. Not yet.

DAY 2: EDIT

Read through your work from yesterday. How does it feel? Was it something you enjoyed? Did you like living in fiction, building a world and choosing two characters to inhabit it? Spend an hour or two editing this short story and rewriting where necessary. Get it to a standard you're happy with. It doesn't need to be perfect. Just something you feel you can make better over time.

DAY 3: RESEARCH AND DEVELOPMENT

Look at old photographs. Read old diaries. Re-read a favourite short story or essay. Soak up the work of others for an hour.

DAY 4: THE PERSONAL ESSAY

Think of a significant moment from the past two or three years, a memory that signalled a turning point. Everything from a break-up to an argument to finally completing *Red Dead Redemption* might count. Zero in on this moment of change. Tell us where you were, what happened, what you were doing or wearing and what the place looked, sounded, smelled and felt like. Who else was there? What was their role in this experience? Tell us about what led to this moment and what it changed within you. Take this as a prompt and write a 1,000-word personal essay exploring the precise moment of transformation or change.

Get that done in 1,000 words and take the rest of the day off. See you tomorrow.

DAY 5: EDIT

It's edit day again, so read through your work from yesterday. How does it feel? Did you enjoy it? Do you like using your life, your opinions, your worldview as a way of exploring a theme? Did you find it an easy task? How much did you struggle? How much did you put on the page? What's missing? Spend an hour or two editing this personal essay and rewriting where necessary. Get it to a standard you're okay with. Again, it doesn't need to be perfect. Just something you feel you can make better over time.

DAY 6: THE FREEWRITE

Today you're going to do a freewrite. Your prompt is: 'Today I feel . . .' Get that at the top of a notebook page and see where the writing takes you. Don't worry about full sentences or a narrative. Don't worry if it becomes a list or a soup of words. Don't worry if it's disjointed or disconnected. Don't worry if you're feeling great and don't think that's particularly narratively challenging. This is about the writing. The recording. The letting your pen do the talking. Don't stop for an hour. See where your pen takes you.

DAY 7: REVIEW

It's review day. Hard to edit a freewrite, but what I would do is read through your work and note down any words, phrases, themes or moments you like enough to keep and use somewhere else.

After this week, you'll have three very different modes of writing. Try to consider which one feels most comfortable and which you would like to continue with.

As we finish Part 1, what I want you to consider is, what feels comfortable to me? Where do I feel most like myself?

Finding your voice is a lifelong goal for most writers. But with these exercises you won't be afraid of writing without consequence, trying different things. The next section gets very technical, and it's more designed for people who have specific stories they want to tell. Meet me in Part 3 if you're still struggling and I'll have some more exercises for you on how to find a way of writing that fits you.

The rest of you, see you in Part 2.

PART 2:

HOW DO I PLAN A STORY?

This part of our work is much more technical than Part 1. This is the bit where we're thinking about the mechanics of storytelling. I've tried to make them apply to as many different forms as I can because I don't know what you're working on. These techniques apply whether you're writing fiction, non-fiction, auto-fiction, memoir, short story or essay. Certain creative writing professors are probably reading this right now and raising their bemused eyebrows so much they are poking planes. But you know what, creative writing professor? YOU'RE NOT MY REAL DAD. I couldn't afford your course and taught myself, so suck it!

Am I projecting?

Sounds that way, huh?

We're going to start with thinking about your voice, developing it and making it your own. Then we'll spend time reflecting on structure, story, plot, character, setting, dialogue and pace. But first, the important voice conversation.

In Part 1, we started wondering about voice in terms of theme, what we want to say and the types of stories we want to tell. Now, I'm going to talk more about how understanding the structures of storytelling can enhance your voice. It's no replacement for your natural instinct. But it can give you the building blocks, or the foundations or even the load-bearing walls for the story (building, ahem, there's a pun here) you have in your head.

*

Just so we're clear, here are some terms we will be working with in this section. **Style** is the mechanical or technical aspect of writing, and is specific to the subject. Style is about execution. **Voice** is about the unique worldview of the author and how that influences their word choice, and the lens through which the story is told and the narrative engine that drives the story forward. **Tone** is about the feeling of the writing. It informs how we feel through the story overall as well as through individual sequences.

Why do I need to tell this story right now?

Voice is about worldview, and worldview has to have an urgency to it. Stories need a reason to happen. Stories that compel readers to commit to a character's interior and exterior worlds require investment and, in order for that investment to be justified, we need to think about the story's reason for existence.

So, ask yourself, for the characters of your story: why now?

You know how in every work meeting ever, there's always that guy – and it is always a man – who doesn't say anything, and at the point of decision, he pipes up and says, 'Can we all just take a step back and think about why we're doing this in the first place?' and everyone gets frustrated?

This is that question.

Turns out that it's an important question to ask. It's best to ask it early on.

'Why now?' is an important question to ask. Because too often we can get hung up on the plot. Sure, the meteorite has landed or a dead body has been found or the huge family bust-up has resulted in a trial separation, but why does this story need to happen right now?

Think about why this story can only happen for this character right now. If life hadn't intervened and they had carried on as normal, what would this have meant? Why is it now that a plot has been triggered?

It's the same for non-fiction, for a personal essay. What is happening in the world that demands that this story be told *right now*? What is it about this untold piece of history, this world event, this personal reaction to something?

Think about it this way: in a lot of fiction, when we first meet our protagonist, they have been living in denial of some sort of dysfunction. They should have left that job, they aren't happy, they are 'content with what they've got', they should have asked that person out, they should leave that person. Whatever the dysfunction is, whatever this vulnerability, this thing stopping them self-actualizing is, they are in denial of it, consciously or unconsciously, or haven't addressed it yet, because they haven't worked out how.

Most protagonists fit into three archetypes.

First, the willing hero who feels they were destined for more, but something has been holding them back until this very moment. Imagine Luke Skywalker, staring at the twin moons circling Tattooine, his boots dusty from working on his uncle's farm, thinking 'damn, dude, there's got to be more to life than this'.

Second, the character who is resistant to change and never wanted to be special (why are they resisting change and what scares them about it? What are they protecting about themselves?). Imagine Frodo, his feet dusty with the muck and rough and tumble of the Shire, deciding that everything he wants is right here and he'll never ever leave.

Finally, there is the one in complete denial, unaware that change, being special, being destined for more, was even an option (what is it about their worldview that is limiting and only serves to hold them back? What will the discovery of the new world give them?). Think Dorothy in *The Wizard of Oz*, who has no idea Oz exists, but as soon as she finds herself there, she has a journey to get back to the place that wasn't so bad – home – helping people along the way.

These three protagonists want/need something completely different.

So, ask yourself, at every opportunity, what do my characters want?

Once you've explored these questions, you need to work out what it is about this very day, right now, that means destiny has other plans for them and crashes into their lives to offer them change, whether they want it or not?

The meteorite, the dead body and the family bust-up are all examples of this moment of life coming at you fast, when you least expect it. What you need to work out for your character is, why now?

If they don't act, will life pass them by? Is this their last moment for happiness? Are they not as content as they realize? Are they destined for more? Do they need to change even though they don't want to? And did they even know change was possible? Two clichés to work into the 'why now' of your story: one is working out what your character wants and what they need. Are these the same thing? Often, drama and conflict require that these things be different.

This approach works for personal essays as well. The personal essay must be led by its instigating moment. What prompted me to tell this story now? What is it about my personal response to a Richard Pryor routine, or the new *Fast and Furious* film, or that time I felt like an outsider in a specific situation that warrants further interrogation?

If you're writing a broader piece of non-fiction, be it creative or much more fact-based, it's worth thinking about what gives the writing its urgency. To give you an example, if I were to write a book about the way we look at work and our relationship with work, I would probably want to position it in response to lessons learned during the first stage of the Covid-19 pandemic, because that acted as a circuit breaker for so much around our relationships with work. Office-based jobs moved home, front-line jobs continued either for the safety or the convenience of others, and many found that their work dried up. I spoke to performers who said that their jobs don't exist anymore, and that ushered in a real existential crisis about their identity because, whether they wanted to admit it or not, their sense of self was wrapped up in what they did.

Whether it's a novel or a short story, an essay or a journalistic piece, a script or a poem, the story not only needs you the writer to decide why you need to write it right now, but the story needs to be charged with some urgency, whether it's through the main actors in the piece or what is happening in the world right now.

So, can we take a step back and work out why now. Why now?

Writing Prompt
(take as long as you need)

Think of a scenario unfolding before your story takes place. An interaction that shows off your character's dysfunction or fatal flaw. Now you're in your story world and everything is changing for your character. Wonder how they might have reacted before your story even starts. Have the characters be in their everyday lives and think about how their flaw is leading to bad decisions. Describe this scene. Make sure they are unaware of what needs to change.

(If you are writing a personal essay or a memoir, pick a time from your own life.)

How do I begin planning my story?

When I start anything, be it a story or a longer book project, I create three new Word documents. One is called EVERYTHING I KNOW ABOUT THIS WORLD (thanks to author and teacher Alice Jolly for this top tip), where I dump everything I know about the world, the precincts and the people in the world. I might write that this takes place in July 2018, during a World Cup match. I might make notes on what's happening politically, what song is on the radio. I might create some characters. I might sketch out the local pub. I may even take photos of streets on my phone, or landscapes that I want to replicate in the book. For the thing I'm currently working on, because it takes place in the world of hotels, I'm putting photos of the types of hotel into the document. Sometimes schematics, sometimes stationary. Whatever I come across. I'm also interested in the backrooms of these hotels, so where I see them on films or photographs, I collect them. This is a living, breathing document. Whenever something crops up, I stick it in.

The other document is my character document. Here I build up what these characters look like, how they dress, what their faces do when they laugh, how they speak. Maybe they talk in questions. Maybe they never say what they're thinking. Maybe they use 'innit' as a full stop. It's useful to know. Again, this is a living and breathing document, because as I get into the draft, things will occur to me. It's important, though, to give some thought to the basics of your characters. What is their major shortcoming? Who do they want to be that is different from who they need to be? What is not working in their life that your story is going to show them is no longer fit for purpose? What are some significant moments in their past? Who are their significant relationships, both positive and negative? What is their living space like? Some of this stuff won't even make it into the final book. But you need to know who the players are.

The third document is my plot document. I already know what the story of my book is but now I need to apply it to a plot. I know what it's about, now to work out what actually happens. I try to keep this document brief. But if I work out a basic roadmap before I start writing, I know where I'm going and it doesn't mean that I'm throwing in random dramatic conflict later on to keep the plot going. Remember: a story can be anywhere between six words and 300,000+. It could be 50,000 words, 40,000, 100,000 . . . there's no fixed way to be. However long it is, it has to have a plot that justifies the reader's investment in reading it. So in this plot document, remember to ensure causality. Action creates more action, creates reaction, creates action, creates conflict, and so on. The plot document is where you will work all this out. You know the characters, the precincts, now . . . give them some stuff to do. Remember, BUT, BECAUSE and WHY when you're working out your plot. He does this, BUT this happens, and BECAUSE this happens, this now happens – WHY did it happen? And so on. Even if you're one of those people who's like, 'dude, I like to work it out as I go . . .', I'm gonna tell you, it only works for some of that first draft. You have to have a roadmap. It doesn't need to be super detailed. But it has to show you why things move the way they do.

Okay, this is us warming up. This is what we need to do before we start writing. You may have the perfect opening paragraph or scene. You might think you know all this. But it's all in your head currently. Get it out of your head. Because in your head, it's perfect and slightly amorphous and abstract. Getting these things down on paper will allow you to make this book actually happen.

I remember meeting someone at a wedding and as soon as he found out I was a writer, he said he was working on a book. I asked what it was about and he said he didn't want to tell me in case I stole the idea. Which was very presumptuous. But hey ho. He then told me he hadn't actually started it yet, but he had the perfect first sentence. I asked what it was, and he told me. It was fine; a good first sentence.

I didn't have the heart to tell him that the first sentence is usually the last thing to think about. You don't always start a story in the right place and you don't always figure out the style till later. And often the perfect first sentence can be your undoing. Knowing that the sentence after won't be as perfect as the perfect first sentence, you might not start. Or you might plough through and be disappointed that nothing sounds as good as that opening.

Writing Prompt: Do All of the Above
(take as long as you need)

Super simple. Create three new documents:

1. EVERYTHING I KNOW ABOUT [THIS NOVEL]
2. CHARACTERS
3. PLOT

Start filling these things out. As much as you can. I would focus on character first, then plot, and as these two are worked out, things will organically be added to the 'everything' doc.

Is this the last story on earth?

When I first started out, I didn't plan. I plunged in to the murky waters. I had a killer first line: 'It was then that Amit decided to start a band.' And I knew it was going to flash forward fifteen-odd years at the end to show how this particular school year made him the person he became, and that was it. I knew I wanted the book to feel like season one of a sitcom and for each chapter to be episodic: get the band together, secure the equipment, ask the girl out, force your mum to take you out clothes shopping, and I knew I wanted it to be funny.

That was it. My first novel, ladies and gentlemen.

It was a very feel-your-way-through mode of writing a book. But it worked because I was writing this like it was the last thing I was ever going to write. I'd written a manuscript before, a fictionalized account of a bizarre year volunteering at a school in Kenya. It had got a few near misses with publishers and agents, but no bites. I was at the end of my tether and all the feedback I'd been given about the book involved starting again. But this didn't feel like the project that I wanted to give my everything to. Increasingly, it felt like a way of documenting and processing the weirdness of the previous year, rather than a book that needed to be on everyone's shelves and be read forever.

It took me a while to realize: if you're willing to do the work you know you need to do, it's a keeper. If not, maybe it's not the one. Sometimes that realization can take a while because you've already invested so much time in the first draft.

That's the thing about writing. Nothing unpublished is thrown away. Writing a full-length manuscript showed me I had the stamina to write something that length. At the same time, I knew that I didn't have much to say that could be sustained across the pages of a book.

I'd like to add that this applies to shorter pieces, like articles, poems, short stories and essays. You can spend ages trying to record something or write it, and when you know the thing you need to do is start again, rather than edit what's already on the page, that can feel horrible.

Some of you might not be at the position yet where you've got any writing down to think about whether you want to put the hard editing hours into it. Stay with me – I have a point to make.

My friend and mentor, Niven Govinden, sent me a book called *Sag Harbor*, by Colson Whitehead. It was a hilarious warm-hearted coming-of-age story about a group of young Black kids summering at Sag Harbor, Long Island in the eighties, running around, playing with cap guns, working in diners, taking the piss out of each other, chasing girls, discovering hip-hop. It was everything I needed to read at that point. It made me think of my own teenage years, my aborted attempts to make myself attractive to girls, my attempts to create a rap band (briefly called The Chemikal Gangstaz), and it made me think of my need to write it all down. My need to record things that happened, to prove they had happened, because if no one wrote about them, time would forget they existed. How when those kids drove that car into that shop, it changed the course of everything at school. How that one dealer in that shopping centre was the single most frightening guy in our entire borough, and how he held my best friend's neighbour to ransom over some weed he'd asked the neighbour to hold while a raid was happening and how the neighbour binned it, scared, when the police spoke to him about suspicious activity. This little suburb needed recording, because these small lives, they said everything about who we are.

When I sat down to write, it felt the only story I could tell but also the only story I wanted to tell. It also felt like the only story I would ever tell. And that meant that everything went onto the page.

There's something freeing about writing something as if it's the last thing you have to say. What amount of self-consciousness can get in your way then? What is there left to feel an imposter about at that stage? I set about writing with no fucks left to give. The only person I needed to service in that instance, in those months, on those pages, was myself.

I felt free.

I'm not going to lie. When I wrote the words, 'It was then that Amit decided to start a band', I knew this was the one. I didn't know if it would ever get published or find a readership. I knew it was the book I was meant to write. The one that all roads had been leading to.

The beauty of such an act of love is that 'It was then that Amit decided to start a band' ended up not being the first line and the flash forward ended up being a framing for the entire novel, all flashing back in the instance of a short car journey. And for all its mistakes, it still feels like it has something special on those pages. I can physically see that I'm a better writer now. But I know where I've come from.

I remember watching Zadie Smith read from *White Teeth*, many years after it had come out. It was between *On Beauty* and *NW* and she was part of a line-up raising money for a theatre in Kilburn. Hanif Kureishi was there too, reading from *The Buddha of Suburbia*. She admitted, walking out onstage, that she hadn't reread the book in about a decade, and reading back the extract she was about to share in preparation for the event, she'd found it excruciating, like it was from a different writer. She winced as she read, made self-effacing jokes about overwritten sentences. But you could see the enjoyment in her face. There was something special on those pages. Enough to see where she had come from.

I think a lot about when I wrote the first novel. Not in that arrogant, sitting here, deconstructing my creative genius way. It was a formative time of my life and I long to recapture the energy I gave that first novel. I long to feel like this is the last story I will ever tell. Because that is a fire-in-the-belly feeling.

So, dear writer friend, now we're getting to know each other a bit: I want to ask you about this thing you want to write, this story. What makes it the last story you will tell? If this was the only thing you ever got to write, could you stand by it and say, it was the only thing I wanted to say and needed to say?

Let's start there.

What do I need to put into a story plan?

I wrote that first novel with only a beginning and end and then had fun filling in what happened between those two points. The writing process around my second novel was different. I tried to plot out all the action in advance. It didn't work. It was a series of 'and then this happens, and then this happens, and then this happens', with zero thought as to *why* it might have happened that way.

Plot is inconsequential if you don't think about the why. Stories aren't like life. In real life, we eat a chickpea curry and cous cous for lunch without consequence. Maybe the reason is, brown rice takes a long time to cook, and we were in a hurry to write this chapter. But is it enough of a detail to put into a book? The irony being that I'm using it in a book to illustrate the type of thing that might not need to go into a book.

We ate chickpea curry and cous cous for lunch. I didn't have time to make rice. My desk was calling.

Not a great detail.

Perhaps, it's more like: Because life forced us to hurry and not take time for ourselves to eat, I cooked a hasty chickpea curry, adding cous cous to the plate, to speed us back to our desks. Where we sat, apart, for the rest of the day.

Now we're talking. Now we know that this is a detail about a relationship. We have the beginnings of story.

Back to my experiments with planning. Writing down the plot did nothing to help me know what the book was or who the characters were or why anything should happen to them or why anyone should care about them.

Stories revolve around characters. We don't read a book for plot, nor do we watch a film for the explosion, nor do we read a poem or essay for the imagery. We are reading or watching for the character's experience, to see the world through their eyes and to let it confirm or contrast with our own.

To plan your story – long or short, fiction or fact – you have to think about character. Who are we following? Why? What makes them interesting enough or compelling enough or vulnerable enough for us to want to spend time with?

We manoeuvre through real life all the time without narration, without a story, without an aim. How I showered this morning is of no consequence. How I slept and what I said to my daughter before I dropped her off at school doesn't matter to anyone but myself. However, to introduce these details into a story requires a reason for the reader to care. Story has to have weight, purpose. The biggest joke about eight seasons of the racist (imho etc.) and compelling television show 24 is that no one ever went to the toilet. 'Wasn't it obvious?' I thought, every time I heard the same boring joke. Why would you show someone going for a piss? In a spy thriller? Unless they let their guard down during said piss and find themselves garrotted to death by the ubiquitous, problematically Brown terrorist baddie. Only for them, seconds later, to be tortured by Jack Bauer. Maybe then you might want to show them going to the toilet. So let's assume Jack went for a wee while we were spending time with the bad guy's human-interest story or enthralled with whatever machinations the evil president was up to.

No one needs toilet scenes unless something dramatic happens in the toilet. Hold all your scenes to the toilet test. Is this akin to reading about someone going to the toilet? What is the purpose of showing us this scene? What is it adding?

The plan, the goal, is the marriage of story and plot. Being in the imagination business, absolutely anything can happen in our stories. That's plot. The bit that resonates with readers, however, well, that's story.

The stuff that needs to go into the plan is what will drive your story forward. We're going to start thinking about planning and structure in the next few chapters. It's going to be a lot of thinking and making notes and going, 'Do I even need this? I'm trying to write a sestina . . .'

I'm not saying that all of what follows is compulsory for a robust story. What I'm suggesting is that it's worth considering before you start, and as you draft, because knowing the structure can give you confidence to keep going, help you out of a hole, or help you second-guess external feedback before you even send it out. So keep all these things in mind as you plan.

The plan you might even end up with is: guy breaks up with girlfriend because she thinks he's a waster. He then wakes up to find a zombie apocalypse has happened. He realizes that in order to win her back, he has to rescue her from the zombies. But in so doing, he takes her to the one safe place she hates: the pub she broke up with him in.

That's the plot of *Shaun of the Dead*, I know. But even this small, super-short plan, plot, story for the film will have considered everything I'm about to go through with you.

What to do when all this stuff feels too hard

Let's pause here for a second.

You don't have to sit and stare at the page right now. That's not always conducive to planning. Thinking about the story shouldn't be a forced activity. Instead of chaining yourself to your desk, go for a walk with a pocket-sized notebook, or do the washing up or fold some clothes. Something repetitive that doesn't require your brain. And run through scenarios. Try to visualize your characters. Try to think about the essence of who they are and the outward nature of who they present themselves to be.

If you have somewhere to be, then take that journey.

I do all my best thinking on trains and buses. I find them soothing. Before attempting any story or essay, I make a playlist of ten to fifteen associated songs that feel thematically linked to what I'm writing about, or might suit the mood, or might be relevant to the time period. Then I get them on my phone and head out on a journey.

I know this may sound like a banal suggestion. Take some time away from your desk and listen to music and let your mind wander. You'd be surprised how often I've suggested this to a writer who feels blocked and they've said, wow, I actually never even thought of that.

I wrote one novel commuting on the coach between Bristol and London. And I wrote another novel on trains while touring the country for *The Good Immigrant*. The forward motion, the patchy wi-fi, the concentrated time when I couldn't be interrupted from my flow by an email or a meeting or a phone call or a colleague asking for help or the internet – every single page on the internet (the Wikipedia holes of, well, this is set in 1930s Cairo, so I should read everything I can find about 1930s Cairo, and 1920s, to be safe). If you could be distracted by it, I was. The train gave me a sustained period to concentrate. And if I stared out the window, or noticed other passengers, it would usually be while I was in the world of whatever I was writing. And that fed into what I was creating. How many of my external character descriptions came from the commuters around me, how many of their irritating habits and phone manners and smells. How many fields of green, passing cities or suburbs or backs of hedges offered the visual buffer for my brain to allow itself to immerse me in the story.

Travelling helped. So many overheard conversations and interactions. On the top deck, you notice more of the street, can see more of your surroundings from a new angle, notice people and places more.

I had a small notebook, in which I noted things as they came to me. Here is an example of a page of observations from the notebook. No context offered:

He thinks 'your pain isn't special'
People like the Tories. How else to explain the way they vote.
Can you decolonize time?
The struggle James Baldwin part 2, 8 mins in: unlettered and
    illiterate in the language of the heart

Life drains

Look at the therapy rooms above games shop

The way windows reflect trees sometimes make it look like

    Galactus is approaching in a thick cloud

Don't be impatient with them when they ask for hope.

Now. All this may seem like nonsense to you. But I can see how all these fragments ended up in a personal essay I wrote about clubbing.

The space my brain had in this liminal place gave me time to think. Not all writing time needs to be spent putting words on a page. Consider the thoughts as well. And how they impact what goes on the page and what goes beneath it. Give yourself time to walk around or press pause or let things wash over you as you ride or stare.

Here are three writing prompts to help plan your work and unblock you:

Writing Prompt 1
(30 minutes)

Take the protagonist of your story on a journey. The mode of travel, the direction they're heading, the symbolism of the journey. Write a short descriptive piece about the journey. What do they notice? What do they do? How do they travel? Where does their mind wander to? Do not stop writing. Keep going for thirty minutes (minimum). If, after thirty minutes, you're finding yourself immersed, keep going until you're done. The smaller you can make everything within the piece: the action, the direction, the movement, the landscape, the better.

Writing Prompt 2
(30 minutes)

Pretend you have a fleeting encounter with your protagonist, be it a coffee shop exchange, or you meet them in the palace of the king, or perhaps they rescue you from the dunes of Mars. Write a journal entry, a proper 'Dear Diary' one, about your meeting. Pick something that feels real to the world you're writing about and the world the characters exist in. Try to figure out the mystery of this character. Try to see what they're like as a person, who do they present as, what assumptions might you make of them having only just met them. If you're writing about a real person, try to imagine your first meeting. The trick is to try to understand how a character might present themselves externally, and how that might make acquaintances feel about them, positively or not.

Writing Prompt 3
(30 minutes)

Take your main protagonist, the one you are trying to figure out. Write a confession for something they have done, be it trivial (yes, I ate the biscuits you blamed my brother for when we were five) or serious (yes, I committed the murder you blamed my brother for when we were thirty-five). Or somewhere in between. Now this is a confession, so you're laying it all on the line. The thing you did, the detailed proof of things only the guilty party could know about the deed in question, why you did it, the justification you used, how it makes you feel years later to confess, and how it felt at the time. If you want to include what or who is forcing the confession, that's great. But the trick of this is to understand how our characters remember things or rationalize things to themselves or others. This is as useful for non-fiction as it is for fiction because it helps us to understand characters beyond the things they have told us or the things we know about them through research or interview. If we're writing this as a personal essay, or diary piece, the confession will help us to understand ourselves in the moment and the way we feel about these things years later after they've been sieved through over time.

Either way, these three prompts should get you thinking about the characters in your story as people with real feelings, hopes, dreams, emotional registers and physical tics. If you're still trying to find your protagonist, then you can try these exercises with a bunch of different imagined characters to see how you like them and how they fit. If you're at the freewriting stage, go wild with these, make them as outrageous and outlandish and unpredictable as you want. This is writing without consequence for you.

Have fun because break time is nearly over.

Why? Why? Why? Why? Why?

We're getting closer to planning your story. Don't you worry. I can feel you revving to go like you're in pole position and one win away from the title.

We're still in thinking phase. This is a precious time. Because, once we start committing things to paper, they become real. They start to become the shape of a story populated by people who deserve to have their story told, demand that their story be told, and who know you're the only one who can tell their story.

What I'm going to suggest below is a good start, but the important thing is to be flexible. In this planning, things will change as you think more and immerse yourself in the story world. And in the writing, things will change again. Being prepared for that will give you confidence in your ability to wrestle with this story.

So with all that said, let's talk about plot and consequence.

Story is the timeline.
Plot is the sequences that drive us down the timeline.

Story is the reason a decision is made, or an action is undertaken.
Plot is the consequences of that decision or action.

Story is cause, and plot is effect.

Story is the reason for metamorphosis.
Plot is the method.

A literary theme is the main idea or underlying meaning a writer explores in a novel, short story or other literary work. The theme of a story can be conveyed using characters, setting, dialogue, plot or a combination of all these elements.

Story relies on characters, setting, dialogue, plot or a combination of all these elements to discuss a theme.

Plot gives our characters choices to make, forcing them to accept or reject the consequences of those choices, and moving them towards a conclusion.

So, armed with the knowledge of what your story is about, you're going to be thinking about what happens on the page. You may know the events because it's something from your life or someone else's. You may be making stuff up, which is the fun bit. The way to marry plot and story, as previously, is to talk about characters, choices and consequences. You've written your plan as per the previous prompt.

Let's go through it again, but think about it in terms of causality. Characters make choices because of things to do with their opinions, their values, their core self-image. Those choices have consequences. Especially if they impact on other characters who also have opinions, values and a core self-image. This is what causes conflict. Conflict drives drama. Conflict can be internal and it can be external. But it has to be there. And because of conflict, we see that consequences drive plot, consequences force characters to reflect on their opinions, their values, their core self-image. Consequences bring the protagonists to moments where they have to think differently about the way they view the world. Consequences put them in a position to change. One way to place choices and consequences into scenes involving characters is to think about how our actions force reactions. And these actions should always be driven by something we hold dear – a value or a belief or something that defines how we think about ourselves and our place in the world.

1. If you know the structure of the novel, you'll know where to speed up and where to slow down. Where a pause, a moment of light relief, a tangent with a secondary plotline, a lingering moment might be apt. And you'll know where it needs to be action, action, action; running, jumping, climbing trees. When you write your synopsis, it's helpful to make a mental note of where you might want to linger or speed up. Often in screenwriting, we talk about the stakes, and raising them. Really, for a novel, you're concerned with what your characters want, and how and when you're going to give it to them or withhold it from them. Planning out the novel can signpost the moments of reflection and the moments of action.

2. The way you write changes when you speed up and slow down the action. Your sentences might be choppier, more staccato, brusque and action-focused when you're upping the action and the tension. There may be more dialogue, but in shorter bursts. When you break into moments of reflection there will be longer, more descriptive sentences, more interior monologue, more reflection and more feeling, more noticing, more seeing.

3. Pace isn't about speeding up and slowing down the action. Pace is about balance. Keeping your reader engaged. If

you're thinking about it in terms of action versus reflection, you're going about it all wrong. Be consistent.

4. Often, consistency in your pacing comes from cause and effect. I've said on page 69 that knowing how your action unfolds using the words 'but' and 'because' ensures you're thinking about action and consequence. How something happens and it causes someone to act and their action has consequences and those consequences result in an escalation of a problem. Simon walks to the park. But the park is closed. So he goes to the pub. Because he goes to the pub, he runs into his friend Mark. Because Mark just got fired, he wants to do a bank heist. But Simon promised his wife he was going to get a regular job now. So they decide to do the heist. And Simon decides to keep his wife in the dark, and Mark, as it turns out, has been waiting for Simon; this wasn't random. Because Simon is the reason Mark got fired. Dun, dun, DUN! Pace! Causality! See how cause and effect is one way of managing pace and story. We have the slow bits, the big bits, the dramatic bits, the revelatory bits.

5. This is the flow of pace, of using choice and consequence to drive plot forward, to make the reader understand why something happens: conflict occurs. Character addresses the external consequences. Character confronts internal consequences. This creates a new reality. New reality brings conflict. Character addresses . . . Etc etc etc. And again, and again and again. The importance of this equation is that it works on a level that dictates every choice, action and reaction of the characters. It's not about if he pulls the trigger, the bomb will slip and the world will explode. It's more a question of if he stops in front of the bad guy and pauses, what will the pause lead to? What are the ramifications of the pause? What happens next, and on and

on? This is an important equation because it roots our characters in moments and forces their interior and exterior to speak to each other.

Imagine this scene, by way of example: Paul and Paula are doing the washing up. They've just finished dinner and they're tidying their kitchen before slumping in front of a shared television programme and having one to five more glasses of wine before bed. It's been a long day at work. A long day for Paul. An even longer one for Paula. We have set the scene. Then Paul drops Paula's favourite mug on the floor and Paula shouts at Paul in frustration, in that moment throwing at him the frustrations of a beloved item broken, the hard day at work and the inherent difficulty between them that causes friction. This is our conflict. Our dramatic moment. Our tense situation. An argument over a mug. This results in an external consequence: Paula leaves the room in frustration, because Paul says the thing that he knows will irritate her, a weaponized barb, designed to sting. (Something like, 'You're just like your mum . . .' or 'You're nothing like your mum . . .' or something else, the worst thing Paula could possibly hear in that moment.) Paula sits on the edge of the bathtub, stewing; the argument escalated by her storming away, the conflict at fever pitch because of the external consequences of their back and forth. An internal resolution forms: I can't be here anymore. I need to leave. And thus, a new reality is created. Paula is leaving Paul. And with the new reality comes more conflict, because Paula is about to tell Paul, and this will result in external consequences and this will result in an internal resolution and this will create a new reality and in that new reality conflict will . . .

You get the picture.

So using pace and cause and effect, the consequence of it all, is how we can keep the plot moving. It can also make us as writers know where we're moving next. Pace is about moving the plot along. Moving the plot along is about ensuring your characters' choices force decisions that move them from one moment to another quickly and with purpose and intention.

Pace is about not lingering in the interstitial boredom of moments. It's about movement. More importantly, it helps readers understand why, why, why, why, *why* anyone does anything.

Writing Prompt 1
(45 minutes)

Think about the main bits of your story in terms of choice and consequence, in terms of but, because and why, in terms of why does this happen and why does this affect the protagonist and how does it affect them? Don't worry about every single decision, but consider the big moments in your story. What is the why why why of it all? What is the but and because of it all?

Writing Prompt 2
(30 minutes)

Now let's do a little experiment to get you thinking about pacing your character through some choices and consequences.

Your character has thirty minutes to run to the shops for something they forgot. Take them on that journey. Throw obstacles in their way. Have them confront those obstacles. What do they choose to do? What are the consequences of their decision? How does this raise the stakes? Do everything you can to stop them getting back from the shops before thirty minutes elapses. This isn't them seeing the road to the shops blocked, so they decide to take the long way round. This is about what happens on the long way round. The reason it's the long way round? Who might they encounter that they don't usually? What's the worst that could happen?

How do I slow my story down so the readers don't get exhausted?

We've spoken a lot about action and cause and effect and momentum and go, go, go, plot, plot, plot, keep the readers reading, but you know what? Stories need to ebb and flow. Quiet bits and loud bits. Like a piece of experimental classical music.

We've spent time establishing a marble run of events to keep the plot moving forward. But the thing about pace, about dramatic tension, about momentum, is that they're hard to sustain, and a reader can tire.

One of the things about those Dan Brown books is, there is so much running, jumping, climbing trees, deciphering maps, getting locked in rooms and following maps only famous iconographers can interpret, that you're exhausted by the end. And sure, you eat it up, you gulp it up, you hoof it all in your mouth like you're a cartoon cat called Tom pouring an entire food mountain into your mouth – so why do you still feel hungry? Action needs pace and pace needs a push-pull feel to it. You want the bits filled with drama and action and choice and consequence to have impact and you want the quiet reflective bits to have resonance.

We're going to take some time to reflect on our characters.

How are they and where do they go during these quieter moments?

Characters need moments to reflect. Moments to take stock. Moments to work out what on earth to do next.

The trick to slowing down the action in a story is to think, how does one take stock? What happens in the quiet moments when no one else is looking? Might we head down memory lane? Might we have a meal, a walk, a sit down, lock ourselves in a cupboard? Often, the writing requires you to force the reflection by following your protagonist's train of thought, having them chew over revelations, turns of events or what they're discovering about themselves. There's a reason why, in *Star Wars*, after the daring escape from Mos Eisley, we spend a few minutes exploring the boredom of deep space travel with an ultra-violent chess game, Luke is processing what it takes to be a hero, and also, is beginning to realize that he can never go home again.

Slow down the action as well as speed it up. Make it interesting, make it thematically relevant, don't make it boring and don't overstay your welcome.

Here are some tips for slowing down the action, in a handy list because, ironically, I want to get through this bit in a hurry rather than draw it out:

1. Slowing down the action isn't about having your character have a fifty-page dinner with their best friends, where you transcribe their/your pet theories/bants about their/your least favourite Quentin Tarantino film or whatever. Slowing down the action is about forcing your character to reflect on theme: what is their thesis, the way they view the world? What is the antithesis of the way they view the world? How has the drama of previous scenes pitted thesis and antithesis against each other? What is the synthesis of this? If you're

in doubt, take them off for a walk around familiar surroundings and have them notice something new.

2. Slowing down the plot isn't the same as writing more description. You're slowing down the action with a moment of revelation for a character. You're not filling the page with more words, preferably multi-syllabled ones.

3. More often than not, this should be a period of solitude for the character. A good way of doing this is often making them the loneliest person in a room filled with people.

4. These quieter scenes should, as per the previous pace equation, result in an internal resolution and a new reality.

5. Give the reader a chance to breathe. Ebb and flow. Not cruise control at top speed. Ebb. And. Flow.

Writing Prompt
(30 minutes)

Take your main character for a walk around familiar surroundings. Describe everything they see. And at the right moment for you and them, have them look at a familiar thing with new eyes. What do they notice this time?

Please, please, please can I write my story plan now because I am ready to goooooooooooo?

Now you're ready to write the plan. God. That took a while, didn't it? A bunch of sections ago, you were like, yes, yes, yes, okay, fine, I hear you Keshula, I'll write a plan. And then we dithered and delayed and planned some more and thought deeper and now a plan actually seems feasible. Right?

Also, don't call me Keshula. I have three nicknames. And you and I? We're not there yet. Also, I'm making a huge assumption that you're a nickname person.

What I want you to do now is make that plan. I'll wait. There you go. That's all this section is about: permission to go plan. Go on, I'll be here coming up with more nicknames for myself.

Now what?

Hey! Nikismo The Magnificent here.

What do we think?

No. I didn't believe in that one either. I'll keep working on it.

Before we get you to write, there are two things to consider.
The first is about this plan we've made. The next is all about that
first draft.

First, this plan is not a dead document. It's not one of those
things you save as [NAME OF STORY]_FINAL. It's a living,
breathing document. It is not being written in isolation, far away
from the writing itself. This is a document that will live and
breathe and grow with your story the more you get into it.
Planning is a roadmap. It's a statement of intent, a depiction of
the big story beats, and it's a reminder of a character's arc and
thematic journey. But also, you're a writer. As you get deeper into
the story, more revelations and discoveries await you. You might
realize that the way they are the way they are is because of a
previous relationship with x, you might find new things about their
antagonists, you might find . . . you might just find . . . that the
plan, the one that came from a novel you wrote in your head,
doesn't work in execution, and you need to switch it up.

The plan, if you write it and put it away – with an intention never to adapt, edit or evolve it – stands to get in your way. Sticking too closely to the plan can drive you to writer's block. Because you have an expectation of where something needs to go and actually it doesn't work.

So what's the point? I made you write the plan, and you're a fly-by-the-seat-of-your-pants writer. Was it all a waste?

Nah, mate, would Nikismo The Magnificent do you like that?

No? Still not working, is it?

No, but seriously. It is an important document. Writing a story requires flying by the seat of your pants and writing to a plan. Both guide you. Neither can get this written on their own. The spirit of creation with the semblance of structure. A well-structured story doesn't always make for a brilliant story. And a creative story, without some reins, can read like a mess.

Treat your plan like a recipe. You have an idea of how it should taste. You know the ingredients. Fine-tuning alone will get it *chef's kiss*.

What is draft zero?

The glorious thing about writing, and writing in drafts, and taking your time is that you are in control of what you write, when you write, and whether you think it's something you want to share with others.

You know when you're in the shower, or on the loo or brushing your teeth and you go into zombie mode, like your brain is buffering while your body does all the stuff it's trained to do. Muscle memory kicks in and magically, you somehow emerge showered and fresh (I'm including cleaning your legs here. Wash your legs. Soapy water running down your legs is not the same as cleaning your legs. I won't accept you've fully showered till you've washed your legs) or with sparkling teeth or whatever it is you can do with your brain not in use but the rest of you getting through this life.

This is the time when my brain is fizzing with ideas. With perfect sentences. With nuanced complicated characters that'll place Person X into a canon of unforgettable narrators. With ways to move plot forward. With the descriptive passages. With the skewering societal commentary. With the observations that pepper so many of our everyday interactions. Like, what's the deal with people who don't wash their legs? If they don't wash their sweaty meat sticks, what else do they not clean properly?

It's a long walk from your shower to your writing space. Whether it's a few steps or a few miles or a few hours. And between the two acts, the one where you give your brain space to breathe and the one where you sit down to concentrate and work hard and not keep refreshing a social media app every twenty words as a reward, your brain engages and becomes active again. And the inner critic kicks in. And the inner critic complicates your thoughts. Forces you to replicate words that sounded perfect rattling around an emptied brain. Forces you to describe a universe conjured while you washed your legs. Forces you to be as good on the page as you know you are in your brain, with no one looking. That's the sly thing about that first draft. It feels like you're looking over your shoulder, tutting at the terrible syntax, unimaginative imagery, basic characters and stagnant plot.

You'll never be as good a writer as you were in the shower.

Welcome to draft zero.

Now, I confess, draft zero is not my term. I don't know who coined it, but I first heard it at the Faber Academy where I teach. Draft zero is effectively the first draft. Whatever you call it, draft zero, draft 1, first pass, it'll be your worst draft, and you won't nail it and some of the syntax will be terrible and some of the imagery will be unimaginative and some of the characters will be basic and some of the plot will be stagnant.

You have to be okay with that. It's your first pass, after all. The first pass is not the final pass. You are in control of when others see this work. You are even in control of how much you look over your own shoulder.

A slippage occurs between brain and page. The idea, perfect in your head, is pushed through a sieve as it is executed. And the way it comes out onto the page is not as good as you thought it would be. This will happen for the whole of draft zero.

Draft zero is about getting the bare bones of a story down on the page. It's easier to refine and edit something than it is to get it right the first time. Also, the more you give your story, in terms of hours and introspection, the deeper the search within the words will get. Repeated passes on the work makes it better. No one is great first time around, especially if it's your first story. We refine and we find the words as we go.

The point I'm trying to make is that you must not be precious about your first draft. Your first draft is about finding the story, getting to know the characters who will help you tell it, getting to understand what makes them tick and what will drive them forward, what obstacles might they come up against that'll cause them some real problems, the interactions they'll have with the rest of the cast of the book, the feel of the novel, in terms of where it's set and what it's tonally trying to do. Characters, story, plot, dialogue, setting. Focus on these things.

Be safe in the knowledge that your understanding of your story will improve with each draft; the clarity of your characters' journey, their arc, their voyage and what they need to go through before they can become the person you want them to be by the end will get reinforced with each pass; the plot, and here I'm including the pacing, the obstacles faced, the problems, the conflicts, will get refined and sometimes collapsed into each other; the dialogue will get snappier, pithier, more entertaining the more you go over it, saying each interaction out aloud; and the setting will become more real the more time you spend in it.

All you can do in draft zero is get the components down in order for you to refine them later. Nothing else matters. Not the opening sentence. Not the closing one. Not the moment of highest tension. Not even that tender love scene in the middle. None of it. All that matters is that you, the writer, get to know who your characters are, what they want and need, the space they occupy, what stands in their way, and who they interact with as they search for the thing that'll give them a resolution, an inner peace, a sense of finality.

Okay, so I have some rules for you to get you through draft zero. Ready?

1. You can edit this once you have finished.
2. Seriously. No editing as you go.
3. Keep a notebook of changes that occur to you as you move through. Keep notes to yourself.
4. I said, no editing!
5. It's okay to add comments to sections with helpful things like 'MAKE THIS BETTER' or 'needs more punch'.
6. Move through this draft. It's a draft, not an edit.
7. Am I hammering this point home enough?
8. Concentrate on character, story, plot, dialogue and setting.
9. Track your plan and adjust as you go.
10. Any stray notes about specificity or research you need to do can wait till after. Have a place to hold all these thoughts.

There you go. The rule is simple: move forward. It's the only way to attempt to write the first draft of a novel.

This is your dump draft, your splurge draft, your 'get everything onto the page while I can' draft. This is the hardest bit. And then the next hardest bit starts, of whipping it into shape. But trust me, it's easier to whip a page filled with words into shape than it is to fill a page with words. We focus on perfection. I only have this limited time to do this, this is a hobby, not my career; it needs to be good enough to show x or y. None of that matters right now. All that matters in this moment is that you were so compelled to tell a story that you actually sat down to write it.

Every subsequent draft is about getting your story further away from you, the writer, and closer to your reader. Draft zero is the shower draft. The draft only you will see. The draft with no consequence.

Who is the inner critic and why do they sound like me?

I have to confess something, and the only way I can frame it is as a weird sort of humble brag. I apologize. But there is a point in its presentation. This is the seventh book I've published, and I'm still freaking out about you reading it. Right now, as you read this and judge whether I know what I'm talking about, I'm sitting somewhere in the dark, hands clamped around my knees, pulling them against my chest, rocking. I'm listening to sad music. Probably James Blake's first album.

I know this is potentially a terrifying chapter to read because we've got you to the point where you're feeling empowered to write. But it would be irresponsible of me to make it seem like putting pen to page makes all the demons go away. The inner critic can't be helped, but you can work with it.

So rather than pretend the inner critic doesn't exist, I want to talk about it, throw light on to it and admit it's there, in the hope that this acknowledgement can help us deal with it.

The inner critic never quietens. And if you can't hear that inner critic, then we have a problem. The inner critic, that part of you that says you're an imposter, you're not good enough, you'll never write a book as good as x or y or z, what's the point, every word feels like a five-year-old wrote it, your plot is more basic than the one times table, it never goes away, and you don't want it to go away. You need to learn how to be in conversation with it. You need to learn how to respond to it and manage it. Because it won't go away. And that's okay. We can live with this little gremlin on our shoulders if we can ensure it is pushing us to be better, not pushing us to stop writing.

The point I'm trying to make about the inner critic is – we give it an outsider's perspective. We compare ourselves unfavourably to writers who have, for all intents and purposes, been edited by an agent and an editor and a copyeditor and been published. People who may have done a creative writing degree or had the support of family, friends, peers. Maybe they've been doing this for a while, in supported environments. They may have come across the right mentors, done things differently to us.

How can we measure ourselves against these writers? I remember at school, a kid constantly wanted our teachers to introduce class rankings. I think he had seen it on a television show and decided, being the type of rich, clever child who needed the validation of being demonstrably better than his classmates, wanted such a thing introduced. But why, but why, but why, the teacher asked him in front of the entire class. You're only in competition with yourself.

This is how you can use your inner critic to your advantage. If your inner critic is you telling you how and when and where to be better, that's good. You know this piece of writing, this story, better than anyone. You know what you want to achieve. Allow the inner critic to hold you to account.

These are the ways to think about your inner critic.

1. It cannot make you as good as another writer. It can only make you the best *you* can be. You don't want to be as good as another writer. You want to be the best *you*.

2. It cannot improve productivity if you focus on what's bad. Frame the things your inner critic tells you as what's good and what could be better. Work on strategies to make what needs to be better better, and what's good, brilliant.

3. Your inner critic can be paralysing. I've seen in workshops, writers consider giving up as a result of receiving feedback from someone that echoes the worst things their inner critic already tells them about themselves. If you know what you need to work on, then focus on it, spend time on it. If your inner critic says your characters lack depth, spend some time developing them. If your plot feels contrived, try addressing that.

4. Your inner critic is not you. It is a self-defence mechanism kicking in. Writing is precious and makes us vulnerable. We're bleeding on the page. Of course, some survival instinct is going to kick in to demand we not do this lest people read it and our most private confessional thoughts be held up to the scrutiny of others.

5. If we are to accept that our inner critic is not us, then we need to remind ourselves that we're not writing initially for our inner critic, or for a scrutinous readership; we're writing for a version of ourselves that needs to read this book. That'll get us through draft zero. After that, we can harness some of our inner critic's energy in the editorial process.

6. Celebrate your accomplishments. You're writing! That's something to celebrate.

7. If we know what our goal is, what our intentions are, accept that this is a vulnerable process, accept that we will have critical thoughts about our work, and know that this will

impact our work, our mental state and the way we treat our bodies, then remember to step outside yourself and take time away from the work, be in the world and remember all the things that made us sit down and bare our souls in the first place.

Writing Prompt: Walk it Off, Friend
(90 minutes)

Go for a walk for one hour around somewhere familiar (if you're able to . . . if not, look through some photographs that have been taken recently). Do this in silence. No noise. No music, no podcasts, no conversation, no phone calls, no social media. Try to notice something new, on the walk or in your photographs. When you come back from the walk, do some freewriting for thirty minutes on the walk, on your thought processes while walking and try to find some significance in the thing you discovered anew.

Do this. And I'll see you in Part 3.

PART 3:

HOW DO I CREATE COMPELLING CHARACTERS?

Character is the most important part of any story. Character is king, and queen, and other important figures that are non-monarchal. Is monarchal a word? If not, it's exactly the kind of thing Keshlaville Shuklaville would make up. Now, *this* is a nickname. I know it works. Because only one person in the world calls me it. And it makes me smile every time. It's unlikely you're that person. Because that person is my good friend Matthew. If you're reading this, Matthew, hi. Also, text me – it's probably been a while.

As for you, yes, what a tangent I went on. But what did we learn in that short little aside about my character? That I like nicknames, that me and my good friend Matthew don't talk as much as we'd like, and that I like to put the onus of contact on to other people.

What does that tell you about me as a character?

We read stories for characters. Novels, short stories, essays, articles, everything. Whether the narrator is a thinly-veiled version of you, or a dude called Fred, we want to feel that a person is on the page. If you're writing a journal entry, you might want to think about how you can appear on the page, and that can develop your writing. If you're writing non-fiction, character is still the toppermost of the poppermost.

If you have characters your readers care about and want to spend time with (whether they like them or not), you can have them do anything: sit in a coffee shop and debate the mundanity of life, or be a knowingly dull academic, or save the world from an asteroid, or chuck a ring down a volcano. With good characters, you can tell personal stories without them seeming overly indulgent. A good character opens up our story.

Building characters can be hard. Because on the one hand, you want to signpost their 'journey'. But that isn't always good to read. You want to hide the character's journey in amongst all their traits, foibles and the rest of it. Most characters start with some flawed vision of who they want to be and they tend to go on a journey that shows them who they need to be. It's the Rolling Stones chorus about not being able to always get what you, you know, want, but sometimes, if you try, it's possible that you'll get what you need instead, innit. So, what is it that your character is protecting about themselves? How is it no longer fit for purpose? How does it limit them? What would make them realize their potential?

So, write down now:

What does my character want?

What do they need?

How do the obstacles I put in their way challenge what they want and present what they need? How do they reject what they need? What is the moment they realize what they need?

Once you have these written down, you'll have the shape of your character's journey. And the obstacles will fit with the plot rather than just be you randomly throwing meteors at the earth. Remember: the meteor in Armageddon represents more than a meteor. But once you have this, you need to make your character feel real.

So write down now:

What happens to my character's body when they are under pressure?

What happens to my character's ability to think logically when they are under pressure?

How do they solve problems? (Imagine them in an Escape Room!)

Who do they turn to in crisis?

This is the beginning of building a character. You need to know their formative memories, significant relationships, biggest disappointments, measures of success, and so on. Even if these don't make it into the text. The above gives you the basics. We'll revisit character in further chapters and try to make them more complex. In the meantime, the above is the foundations.

Now start building them up in terms of what they look like, how old they are, how they dress, what their body language is. Be specific. What is their hair like? Are their eyes always searching, or are they seemingly always stoned? That kind of stuff. What does their smile do to their face? Do they smile? Do they wear jewellery? If they do, as a performance, or because it means something?

A writing tip from Matthew Salesses's essential *Craft in the Real World* was to write the words 'they're the kind of person who . . .' and keep going until you run out of things to write. And these may be habits or personality traits or more surface things. They can be core to their sense of self or esoteric. But they can help with the whole scattergun-get-it-down of it all.

So, like . . .

They're the type of person who never gets up when their alarm goes off. They need twenty more minutes.

They're the type of person who reads the first two and concluding paragraphs of articles by the same three columnists in order to form their opinions.

They're the type of person who cycles to work.

They're the type of person who lets texts from their mum go unreplied to.

They're the type of person to never complain to your face, directly.

They're the type of person who thinks Christopher Nolan films are super-smart and morally superior to everything else.

They're the type of person who only reads one book a year. A non-fiction 'ideas' book.

See? We can build up who these people are through these stray thoughts about routine, opinions, their everyday, their dress, their sense of self. It gives us opportunities to dig in. Why don't they reply to their mum? Why do they form their opinions by waiting for the opinions of others? Why do they never complain to your face, directly?

Before we get to the building up of our characters, let's do a short exercise that puts who they are on their feet a bit so you can experiment with moving them around a space.

Writing Prompt: Party Time, Excellent
(1 hour)

Your main character has arrived at a house party. They don't want to be there. But they went anyway. Spend a minimum of 500 words exploring their experience of the party. When do they arrive? What do they see and do and eat and drink and who do they talk to and not talk to? What happens to their brain and their body? When do they go home? Do they go home? Do they go home alone? You have an hour.

Who are the characters in my story?

A story needs characters to tell it. What follows is a tussle between the characters and their story. We can ask ourselves many questions about our characters, like what they want and what they need and how we can use the story to get them to both of those points. But the simplest point to start at is the question: who are you?

There are, at the very basic, uncomplicated level, three types of protagonist.

The Oblivious Protagonist: This is the protagonist who has no idea change is possible, that there is a bigger world out there, that another version of them is possible. Imagine Dorothy in *The Wizard of Oz*. She is a tourist in Oz, constantly learning the rules of the new land. Her one desire is simple: she wants to find the wizard . . . because? Because, because, because . . . etc. Well, she wants to go home. And that's it. She'll become braver as she goes on through the movie. But the reality is she spends much of the movie moving past her obliviousness. This type of protagonist is rarer than most. I'm not a fan of this as an archetype.

The Pro Protagonist: They are willing and able and waiting for their chance. They know that change is possible, and that there is a bigger, better world out there. They know they are destined for more. Remember Luke Skywalker in *Star Wars: A New Hope*? The young, angel-faced farm boy staring at the twin moons, wishing he could be amongst the stars, and he is destined for adventure and space travel and the universe is going to say, look, if you want change, if you're willing to go on this journey, sure, but it's gonna be life or death, and at the end of it, the prize is . . . you get to save the galaxy.

The Resistant Protagonist: This is the protagonist who knows change is possible but is unwilling to entertain it. They're happy with what they have. They're 'happy'. They've effectively settled for managing that thing that they need changing in their life, be it an unhappy marriage, a boring job, a job as a miner desperate for a holiday on Mars. Imagine Frodo, happy in the Shire, unwilling to leave the Shire, must leave the Shire to save Middle Earth by chucking a ring into a volcano. He will learn something about himself that he can bring back to the Shire and then look at familiar surroundings with new eyes.

All of these protagonists are rationally protecting something about themselves, whether they know it or not. There is a weakness in them. Screenwriters refer to this as a fatal flaw. But I think this is too simplistic. It's not always a flaw. It's not always a position of weakness. Often it's a self-image problem. The way that a character views themselves in the privacy of their own space, when all they have to judge themselves by is the image staring back at them in the mirror. That thing they rationally protect, it has served them well so far. And usually, the universe decides enough is enough and intervenes. And this is usually when the story starts. But the story starts a long time after our protagonist has put barriers up and self-defence protocols in place. Let's work on these before we get to the plot points of cosmic intervention and trigger points and methods of attack.

Because when we meet our character, the point at which our

stories start, they're not a blank slate. In all the years before the start of the story, they have put defences in place. They have endured trauma and pain, life events and relationship fallouts, which have resulted in them being the way they are. And the way they are is often the thing they hide from most people, except the reader. As a writer, keep in your back pocket the worst thing anyone could say to our character. We'll use that in a second.

But first, imagine this: At a character's core, there is their self-image. The thing they think about themselves. Knowingly or not. The long dark night of the soul. The Dorian Gray painting. The rot they know to exist in their core. The trauma they need to get past. The thing that stops them being who they're meant to be. Decades of life have built this up and ratified it and proved and given it reason to exist. As we write, we go outwards, towards how they act in public, the protective rings can get softer and more susceptible to external pressure and as each ring is disrupted by obstacles and conflict, we get closer and closer to addressing who they are at their core. Only then can they challenge who they are.

Self-image: This is what they really think about themselves. The thing that keeps them up at night. This is the thing they are either consciously or unconsciously protecting about themselves. The thing they don't want to deal with. More often than not, they don't know this about themselves yet. It's buried so deep that it's going to take a lot to unpick and get past. What is their sense of worth? What is their biggest fear? What do they despise about themselves? For example, imagine your self-image is *I am weak; I am a weak person.*

Core belief: In order to protect your self-image, you have to constitute a vision of the world that means you don't have to deal with it. Your core beliefs are about how you view yourself, other people and the world. How you all work in relation to each other.

So if you feel weak, then your core beliefs might be you cannot do anything right. And other people are out to catch you out.

Value system: Values guide our behaviour. Our core belief is how we view ourselves and our value systems dictate how we present publicly. So what do we value and hold dear? What do we think is worthless? Values are our standards for what's good and just in society. If you feel you are weak, and that means you cannot do anything right, you might value the opinions of others over your own; you might consider your own opinions to not be worth anyone's time.

Attitude: Our value systems feed our attitudes, how we present ourselves in society. What we are willing to do and what we are not. If values guide our behaviour, then attitudes are the response to our values. They are our likes and dislikes of things, people and objects. If I consider myself to be weak, and my core belief is that I cannot do anything right, and other people are out to catch me out, and my values mean I value other people's opinions over my own, my attitudes might be formed by my personal experiences. I might hate conflict, want everyone to be happy and hate arguments, because arguments result in tension, and tension results in right and wrong – and I don't want people to tell me I'm wrong.

Surface thought: How does this feed into surface thoughts? These dictate my actions, fuel my choices. These are facts I have decided based on my personal experiences. So, if I consider myself to be weak, and my core belief is that I cannot do anything right, and other people are out to catch me out, and my values mean I value other people's opinions over my own, my attitudes might be formed by my personal experiences and I hate conflict, I want everyone to be happy and I hate arguments, because arguments result in tension, and tension results in right and wrong and I don't want people to tell me I'm wrong, then my opinion is that I am not going to tell my friend what I thought of the film in case he has a different opinion to me and I feel stupid.

So to track it back the other way, using one of my prompt responses from earlier – 'he's the type of person to never complain directly to his friend's face':

- I'm not going to tell my friend what I think of this film because I don't want to chance him having a different opinion to me. (SURFACE THOUGHT)
- I prefer peace. I hate conflict. I want everyone to be happy. Arguments cause tension and make me feel stupid. (ATTITUDE)
- I value other people's opinions over my own. I tend to listen to the last opinion I heard. (VALUE)
- I can't do anything right. I feel stupid and people are out to catch me out. (CORE BELIEF)
- I am a weak person. (SELF-IMAGE)

Now, try to work out how that self-image came about. Does it link to a particular relationship or memory? Something in their blood, bloodline, lineage, relationship with parents, a significant other, a time they fell down a well and were haunted by the ghost of a child Lassie couldn't save? Why do they consider themselves weak? Who has been making them feel this way all this time? (Clue: with shouts to Larkin, it's usually the parents, cos they fuck you up etc.)

So, to put this on its feet, let's apply it to a character we all know and love. We all know Spider-Man's mantra, that with great power comes great responsibility. It's the thing his uncle Ben told him and because he feels partly responsible for his uncle's death, he holds it very dear. But before we get to Uncle Ben's death and the birth of Spider-Man as a hero, we have to interrogate who Peter Parker is based on these levels.

Self-image: Peter sees himself as weak, both physically and emotionally. He cannot stand up to bullies, he cannot be seen to let his guardians, Aunt May and Uncle Ben, down. He cannot be one of the kids. He essentially sees himself as worthless. But the reality is the world seeing him as weak and him seeing himself as weak are terrifying, so he hides in his studies.

Core belief: Hard work can mask his inadequacies. Which is why he does well in school and does work around the house for his aunt and feels the compulsion to take on a job to earn money and when he eventually becomes Spider-Man, the hero, he is motivated by a greater sense of hard work and the impact it can have.

Value system: Saving people who cannot stand up for themselves, fighting crime and criminals, ensuring that the law is the law and that strong people do not take advantage of those they see as weak. His standards for what's good and just in society are pretty clear-cut. Don't do crime. Stay in school, and so on.

Attitude: Here's where we get to our big conviction: with great power comes great responsibility. This is his big belief. Because he has seen what he can be responsible for if he isn't responsible. And he has been given this gift. He has to use it.

Surface thought: The Green Goblin is a baddie, let's take him down. (I'm being overly simplistic here – obviously, the best criminals are the complex ones, who think what they're doing is the right thing whether or not they are doing it in the right way.) But it's an important thing: the Green Goblin, by the standard of Parker's core beliefs and his inner value system, and his feeling that ultimately, he is weak, is a baddie.

So this is where we meet our character, at the very start of this thing we're working on. That's where they need to be. They are irrationally protecting something about themselves. And for Peter Parker, the weight of responsibility and his feeling that ultimately he is weak means that he causes more problems for himself: he cannot juggle school and work and home life and social life and love life and dating life and heroism. Something has to give. And he will always be doomed to repeat these mistakes until something changes. Until we get to *The Amazing Spider-Man*, issue #33. But we'll get to that. Let's start from this point. We know that our character is irrationally protecting something about themselves that is no longer fit for purpose. So, what next?

Writing Prompt
(1 hour)

Take a few characters from the book or TV show that you love. Try to analyze them through the above prompts. Start with surface opinions and work your way through them. So: surface thought > attitude > value system > core belief > self-image.

Take characters like Ross and Rachel from *Friends*, or Scrooge and Bob Cratchit from *A Christmas Carol*, or Phil and Grant Mitchell from *EastEnders*, or a superhero, or Connell and Marianne from *Normal People*.

Work through this exercise and see if you can spot what makes them different and what makes them the same. How does their sense of self sit with the other person? Is it a case of opposites attract? Or the old superhero/villain cliché of 'We're not so different, you and I?' Or is there something deeper going on? Use the work of others to try to position these people next to each other. You have an hour.

Who else, besides my main protagonist, is in this story and why?

Relationships drive stories forward. Who are the people your protagonist has relationships with? Who helps, hinders, guides, humours our main character? A protagonist in isolation, the whole 'man vs World' thing, can be boring and static. A great roster of side characters to rely on can inject energy into your story.

Let's take some time to figure out the major relationships in our story protagonist's life. Who else is in their lives? Who are the other characters? Do they get on? Do they not get on? Why don't they get on? Why do they get on? Conflict is everything. It shows us who our characters are under pressure.

List all of the characters around your main character. Do they like the main character? Does the main character like them? Write the specific event/s that caused them to like or dislike each other. What needs to change in their relationship?

Who are these characters? Every character should exist on the page like there is another story somewhere being told with them as the main character. We should know enough of them to not see them only as people who drive this particular story forward. In order to tell you this, I want to tell you the story of the checkpoint officer.

Imagine a book where two people fall in love, their parents aren't happy, society doesn't wish for them to be together. And they do everything they can to not be together but the universe demands that they be together. So they make a decision: they're going to leave.

We witness their daring escape in the middle of the night. How he is nearly discovered helping her down from her first-floor window. How she has forgotten something precious to her. How every moment gives them both individual pause to work out whether this is the right thing to do or whether it's easier to stay. They leave their town and head for the next one. However, there is a checkpoint between them and freedom. We are here, at the tensest moment of the novel, as they stop at the checkpoint.

It's the middle of the night and the checkpoint officer is brusque, difficult and officious. He pores over their documents; he asks them difficult questions; he makes an excruciatingly long phone call out of earshot. And finally he returns. The boy's papers need renewal, but just this once he can go through.

We all breathe a sigh of relief. Wow, this couple, they are free. They leave the blunt, difficult, officious checkpoint officer and run to freedom. The checkpoint officer disappears off the page, merely a passing phantom designed to cause some last-minute drama for our main characters, to make their escape seem more daring.

Except . . . what of the poor blunt difficult officious checkpoint officer? Who is he? And why is he so brusque and difficult?

I put it to you that it's important to consider the story of this pivotal side character and put enough on the page to make them real. Otherwise his bluntness is a plot point, a constructed one where he exists only to provide one final obstacle to our lovers. Be it fiction or non-fiction, the people on our pages need to exist in their own pages. Their story matters.

So, why is he so blunt? He's tired, he's switched from days to nights, maybe his son is getting into trouble and he has been criticized for always being slack with him, always letting him bend the rules, not taking parenting seriously. Maybe he and his partner argued; maybe his mum told him he is nothing like his dad, or just like his dad. Maybe he got a disciplinary for sleeping on the job. Or a text from a mate that his football team lost. All of these things might create a certain energy that he brings to his interaction with a young couple wanting to cross a checkpoint in the middle of the night.

You need to know this stuff. It carries weight to his character. He does not solely exist to make a plot thing happen. He exists in his own right and it's his own personality that makes him brusque and difficult and officious.

Now consider the people around your protagonist, their friends, colleagues, family members. How have they ended up the way they are?

The overly critical boss: what has brought that energy to them? The toxic parent. The passive-aggressive sibling. The chaotic friend who brings mischief to your door. Consider all of these things. Why are they this way?

Writing stories is an act of empathy, not an act of judgement. We cannot present someone's behaviour accurately in a story unless we make an attempt to understand it. People should be afforded complexity. It's up to the reader to make judgements. You may be writing an article about a council member who took a bribe in order to gift a lucrative contract to a company. Unless we try to understand that council member, they are a cookie-cutter baddie. Do we want to read uncomplicated stories about cookie-cutter baddies? Do these count as stories, or judgemental rants?

We must consider the humanity of all the people we write about. Whether we wish to afford them this or not, most people, in stories, think that what they're doing is justifiable in some way. Their reasoning may be flawed, or it may be misguided, or even selfish. But they will have a reason. People in stories who act for evil's sake only, are they interesting to read? Does their proximity to our main protagonist and their journey give us enough story?

So, consider the backstories, the motivations, the self-image of everyone in the story.

Because often, who they are and why they are and their proximity to our main character can tell us a lot about the main character. No one exists in a vacuum. We are shaped by events and problems and successes and opportunities and our environment and our personalities. But we are also shaped by the people around us.

So when in doubt, remember the checkpoint officer.

Now you know what their relationships are with each other, start thinking about their relationship with themselves. Make a list of all the things they like and dislike about themselves.

Now write this: what is the worst thing someone could say to your character? How would they react?

Complicating your characters is about seeing how they cope when life has other plans for them.

Now you know about their motivations, relationships and desires, now start filling in their lives.

Write down:

Their earliest memory

What their dream job would be and what's stopping them from getting it

The first time they met their significant other (if applicable)

A time when they tried their hardest but didn't succeed

What they do on weekends

Habits they have when they think no one is looking

What their hands do when they're happy, sad, angry and frustrated.

Writing Prompt 1
(20 minutes)

Your main character can't sleep. Think about them in their bed. Describe the bed, what they can see in the dark, who else is in the bed (if there is someone), and why they can't sleep. Try to home in on what their body does. I know it sounds creepy, but imagine what they look like when they're sleeping. What position makes them comfortable, where the sheets are, and how they try to blank out the dark thoughts. Do this for twenty minutes.

Writing Prompt 2
(20 minutes)

Think of a side character in your story. Either the best friend or a family member. Do a freewriting exercise imagining their morning. Put yourself in their world and try to see everything from their perspective. If you're writing about a real person, this is where you might marry fact with fiction and opinion. See the world through their eyes. Specifically, write a scene, or a morning, before they arrive in the story you're telling.

Are my characters relatable?

One of the most frequent rejections I used to get about my work was that the characters weren't relatable. Which I found difficult to understand. These are people going through very familiar things: falling in love, yearning for something more than what they had, falling out of love, losing loved ones, trying to be better, failing to be better, trying to better their circumstances, getting past their self-delusion, living their lives.

And yet, they were found to be unrelatable.

I spent years trying to unpick this because, ultimately, I wanted to write better characters. More in-depth characters. More relatable.

Which is when it dawned on me.

This . . . is an impossible task. To make our characters relatable. Relatable to whom? I didn't relate to Emma in Jane Austen. I saw in her a teenage impetuousness and self-delusion that chimed with who I was as a teenager. I didn't relate to Bram Stoker's Dracula. Hate the sight of blood, and it doesn't have the effect on me it does on him. I didn't relate to Adrian Mole, much as I found him funny and calming. Mostly because Adrian Mole's teenage experience wasn't mine. Mostly because I couldn't understand why he did what he did. Did I relate to Jeeves? To Wooster? To the posh, tra-lalala, lashings of ginger beer adventure kids in Enid Blyton stories?

What does 'relatable' mean when it's used in meetings of editors who make decisions about what gets published at their publishing houses?

I've experienced what a few of those editors think it means and how relatability is deployed. So, let's unpick the two for a second.

Relatability is about a shared understanding of what it is to be human, right? It's about using characters and their stories to tell us something about ourselves and the world. Relatability is about creating characters interesting enough, complex enough, entertaining enough, to carry us through a story. It's about a character we're either rooting for or against, or even a character we want to spend time with. Characters who occupy a space that interests us. Characters who give us an insight into a perspective we've not encountered before, or an embodiment of the way we view the world now.

Relatability isn't about seeing yourself in a character, necessarily. It's about noting the choices an author makes in putting a character onto a page and engaging with who they are.

The way the concept of relatability is used often comes down to whether we can see ourselves in different characters. I think this is a distorted way of looking at things. 'Relatability' is often used as a barrier. Male readers say they don't relate to a female character, white readers say they don't relate to characters who aren't white. This is an extremely weird way to admit to not being able to experience the humanity of people who aren't like you, and it's also a dismissive way of engaging with a work.

The way relatability has been wielded against me throughout my career has often been about the characters not being white. An agent told me that the characters in my book were great, but there was no 'story reason' for them to be Asian, which thus meant they weren't relatable. If I'd renamed these characters Bill, Ben and Paula, then perhaps this agent would have related to them hard. But to say that there wasn't a reason for them to not be white and that made them less relatable? That was a big problem. Not only was it a failure to engage with my work, my choices, my craft, it was also a failure to engage with my humanity.

Another time the way relatability was used against me was in the note 'I don't relate to these characters and it makes it hard to love them'. This was from an actual editor! Of actual books! About made-up worlds! This same editor had edited books featuring witches! And magical beings! And middle-aged, middle-class white male creative writing professors who sleep with their impossibly attractive younger students and then are sad for four hundred pages! And my boys, my teenage boys, my idiot teenage boys trying to muddle their way through school and work out who they are, woah . . . unrelatable. This meant, to me, I don't think I am the audience for the book and therefore won't engage with it, which is actually an easier rejection than a nonsense note about relatability.

So, what do we do with all this stuff? How does it feed what we write and how we present people on a page? The first thing is to consider that the reader always brings themselves to every reading of what you do. Which means they project on to you, your words, your stories, your characters, your themes, their lives, their foibles, frustrations, ignorance, blind spots, biases and intentions. It's not helpful. There is no such thing as a neutral reading. And you don't want a neutral reading. You want to create some emotion in your reader.

But knowing that they'll project on to their reader what they will is a freeing thing. It reminds us that we cannot control how someone else reads our story, what they may read into it, what they may see and miss. All we can do is honour the intentions we established earlier.

We should also lean into the space where unrelatability meets specificity and write for our intended reader, our implied audience. Because ultimately, they are the ones who want to read this story. Not everything is for everyone and that's okay.

We are looking to connect with our intended reader, of course, but we are also looking for readers who don't have an expectation or a block about connecting with characters who are nothing like they are. There is so much out there to read and to watch, so write for the people you know want these stories.

What do my characters want?

Big question! What do they want?

All our characters have to want something. It can be something as easy as money. Think about Del Boy in *Only Fools and Horses*. What he wanted was the catchphrase of the entire show: 'This time next year we'll be millionaires.' Or it might be power. Or it might be to perform a just act, like rescue someone or destroy something or find someone.

All our characters have to have a specific want in the story. And the best stories are when our specific wants conflict with the wants of other characters. A want has to be specific. Ultimately, we all want to be happy and comfortable and secure and all the rest of it. But that want, that desire, provides no reason for the story to start right now. So, think of a specific want.

Think of the difference between: 'I want to be rich' and 'This time next year I want to be a millionaire.' One is woollier than the other. One has a specific number and ticking clock, a specific vision of what being rich looks like to them and when they'd like to get there. It's a mantra, a thing to aim for. It's specific. Wanting to be rich brings into question things like how rich and when and what does rich mean for one person and does it match with what another might think?

Nothing moves a story quicker than a specific want, especially if it has a quantifiable engine behind it. Because (not to issue spoilers on a sitcom that hasn't been on the air in the past twenty-odd years!) when Del Boy and his brother Rodney do become millionaires, in the 1996 Christmas special, and finally get what they want, it's amazing. Twenty years have led to this. And it's worth it. Their want spanned fifty-odd episodes over a decade and a half, a lot of near misses, a lot of trials, tribulations, being skint, having quick-get-rich schemes that aren't as they seem, and then, they get it; they get what they want – they are now millionaires.

However, in 2001, when the sitcom was revived, no one wanted to see a show about millionaires. These characters are fighters and grafters and the least interesting thing you can do is to give them what they want. So, when we catch up with the Trotters, years after their good fortune, we see that they have squandered everything and are right back to where they started, back in their flat on their Peckham estate that never stopped being home. This works to jumpstart the narrative. Now that the characters know that becoming millionaires is achievable, they have every reason to try to get back to what they briefly had.

What does your character want? What do they think they'll gain by achieving it? What will they lose? What will they sacrifice for it?

Hover here for a second. Write it down, put it in a voice note. You can refine it to something as pithy as 'this time next year we'll be millionaires' later. First, give it to me unfiltered. Your character can want many things; most people do. But in order for the story to start, they need to have one very present, very specific desire. What is it?

Desire is jet fuel, desire drives story, desire moves someone forward. If the characters in our stories don't want anything, then they won't move forward. Even a character wanting nothing is a story driver. Because they want things to remain as they are. And a story in that context would only exist when things are changing around them in a way that's beyond their control.

We want to write stories that move forward, that keep us reading, keep our readers engaged. And a sure-fire way to do this is to identify what our protagonists long for and what stands in their way. One obstacle after another. One foot in front of the other.

What do my characters need?

I'm going to remind you of earlier, when I paraphrased a famous
song. Remember? The chorus of the Rolling Stones song is the
perfect way to illustrate this section and the difference between
want and need, between desire and actualization. And let's just say,
I can't type it out because it'd cost more money in permission fees
than I have in the world. You know the one I mean though *winky,
smiley face, side-eye the lawyer standing over me*.

God, imagine if you were reading this and not knowing which
Rolling Stones song I meant? You were like 'How is Ruby Tuesday
going to make my character bang?'

There is a classic plot device, a story device, where what our
characters want is not actually what they need. The character's
desire is a McGuffin. Most sitcom plots revolve around a character
wanting something desperately, working hard to get what they
want, getting it and realizing it's not what they expected, usually
then finding it trumped by what they need.

A character is desperate to get the date with the object of their
desire, not realizing that it is their best friend who secretly loves
them. And then they do everything to get the date. And it turns
out the date is a massive butthead and then at the point of
humiliation, who's standing there but the best friend they needed

the whole time. I mean, this is the plot of every high school sitcom. They think the person they've put on the pedestal is the person they want, the person who will make them happy. Instead, the person they are able to be themselves with – the person who is always there – they're the route to happiness.

Keep in your mind what your characters actually need. And actually, what your characters tend to need is something they can only accept once they've exhausted every other option. The thing they need is not to be found on the well-trodden path. It's on the overgrown lane, usually haunted by ghosts of the past. You know? Hedgy Ghost Lane.

Think of the story this way:

My character wants to be a millionaire next year.

My character actually needs to realize that a strong, stable and loving family is worth much more to them than mere money. And sometimes, the struggle, the hustle, when you've got your brother and your idiot uncle and Raquel, that makes the fight much more meaningful than the monetary prize. We don't watch *Only Fools and Horses* to learn how to acquire millions. We watch for the plucky idiocy of two brothers who only have each other. And no matter what happens, they'll always have each other. Isn't that worth more than millions of pounds?

I'll move on from *Only Fools and Horses* now. But it's an important lesson: what our characters want is not always what they need, and you, as the author, you need to know that. We all have a person in our friendship group who offers unsolicited advice, regardless of whether we asked for it. You'll say, my leg hurts, and they'll give you a million solutions, prognoses and suggestions of treatment. When all you want to do is tell them your leg hurts. Our friend thinks we want advice, but we want them to listen.

Remember that scene in the film *White Men Can't Jump*, when Gloria and Billy are lying in bed, sleepy, and Gloria says she's thirsty. Billy springs up, ever the eager-to-please puppy dog, and gets her a glass of water. She's annoyed. She didn't want him to get her water. She wanted him to understand what she's saying. To empathize. To know that he understands her thirst as he has too been thirsty. Later this argument becomes about whether, when he's listening to Jimi Hendrix, he's hearing Jimi. It's a character trait. Billy takes everything at face value and thus is very reactive, rather than taking a beat to understand the severity of the problems in his life and come up with a long-term strategy. It's why he spends the majority of the film hustling little bits of money for playing basketball, and losing it, because in that life, it's easy come easy go. That won't get him out of his jam with the gangsters chasing him. Nor will it mean he ever understands his girlfriend. Or Jimi Hendrix. Billy is befuddled by Gloria's argument. She said she was thirsty. Surely that means she wants a glass of water?

No, she needed him to understand. She wanted him to understand. Then she wanted him to get her some water.

Your job as an author is to empathize and understand what your protagonists need, and how they have ended up in the position they're in. You know what they need and you understand what they want, and you will get them the glass of water, eventually. Just as soon as you've understood and empathized with how they got so thirsty in the first place.

Writing Prompt
(30 minutes)

Write a short story about something you wanted as a teenager. It could be something emotional like love, or to be noticed by a family member, or to not feel anxious every time you took a test. It could be something material, like a t-shirt or a record or something a friend had that you didn't. I want you to remember: what it was like to want it; what you thought it might bring you; and how you hoped it might change your life. And I also want you to remember how you felt when you didn't get it or when you did get it. What changed? What didn't change? Did it make you happy? Was it what you expected? If you didn't get it, did you feel left out or unhappy?

Write for thirty minutes on this and give us the detail of the emotions.

What are the three most important moments in a character's arc?

When we construct character, we talk about their arc a lot. You can find a fun Kurt Vonnegut talk online where he discusses the shape of a story. One of my favourite is 'Man in Hole', which he describes as person gets into trouble and gets out of trouble and is better off for the experience.

A story arc is the shape of a story. It's how we visualize a character moving through a story and experiencing enough so that by the end they have changed or realized something, for better or for worse. They are different. Their worldview is different. They have made the world different.

One way of looking at the arc of a story, the shape of it, is to understand structure and how that can help us. This next bit is very technical. Don't worry, though. I'm going to be here to walk you through it slowly, and in a way that gives you space to look at what you're doing.

We need to recognize that external events in the character's world are as important as the character you start with. These external events can shape them and break them apart to put them back together again. Structure is there to help with the emotional journey of your main character.

I think the three biggest components of structure are the attack point, the mid-point and the low point. I'm going to explain what they are and why they're important. And once you know what they are, you can choose to use them or not.

The attack point, the mid-point and the low point are of critical importance in storytelling. Their function is to pit our protagonist against the world. Even if we're talking about a personal essay or a piece of non-fiction, these story points help. They establish our protagonist's relationship to their surroundings.

The way to construct a story isn't 'oh here's an attack point' and then on page 150 of my 300-page story, or on word 1,500 of my 3,000-word story, 'here is the mid-point', and so on. I don't buy into the writing books that demand an inciting episode at the top of chapter three or on page fifteen of a script.

Same with non-fiction. It needs to be characterful and thinking within the character lines can sometimes help you work out what to put on the page and what to omit.

These points of entry for the universe around the character don't have to be ridiculously high stakes, like the world is ending, or the corrupt president has to be brought down. Instead, these entry points revolve around what's important to the world of the protagonist. Sometimes the protagonist wants to ask someone out on a date or get their dream job or own a pet. These goals can be powerful enough to drive a story forward. Sometimes recording the event, the confession and interrogation, can be enough to drive a story forward. You don't need to excite us with false jeopardy and action; it needs to be important enough to the main character to take them on a journey of discovery, either inwards or outwards, but ultimately inwards.

The Attack Point: Sometimes this is known as this inciting incident. I like to think of it as the moment external forces attack the carefully curated world of the protagonist. It happens early on.

Its purpose is to show the protagonist that the way they've chosen to live their life, either in ignorance of their true potential or in wilful deference to their true potential, is no longer fit for purpose. In fiction, it's a moment of instability, either big (meteorite) or medium (redundancy) or small (they miss the train). What's most important is what happens next, because this is where the story is formed. Have your protagonist grapple with how their life has been destabilized. Have them act in a way that involves taking the easy way out. Have that easy way out build to a bigger problem that sets up the predicament they'll be running from/towards for the rest of the story. But how they're attacked is crucially important.

The attack point is the moment the story starts. A story has to start at a particular time and that particular time needs to not be coincidental. There has to be no other option than for the story to start the moment it does. And usually, the story starts just before the action point. We're back to the question: why now? This time, we're asking for the characters in your story: why must it start right now? Why could it not happen tomorrow or in an hour or last week or four years from now. Why is it that here and now, at this moment, the universe decides enough is enough and it's time to cosmically meddle in someone's life to stir them into action and a voyage of discovery, either within or outside?

First, you establish the flow of their life. The story hasn't even started yet. The character is living their life, protecting themselves from the world, from discovering what they think about themselves. The attack point is usually the point at which external events intervene. Your protagonist's life is attacked by the universe: they lose a job or their parent phones them after fifteen years or they get stopped by the police or they meet the person of their dreams in an elevator. Whatever it is, the encounter must be external and it must push their life into a period of instability. They don't know how to wrestle their lives into control. They are in some sort of free fall. What happens, though, is that they try to take the easy way out, which is human. This is usually where they make things worse. No easy way out now.

The Mid-Point: This is an important part of your character's development. The first half of your story is spent dealing with the attack point and the instability it has caused. However, in trying to re-stabilize and re-calibrate, your character is going to start to see that how they've been living their life no longer suits them. The mid-point is how they're going to go from being reactive to the shock to proactively seeking resolution. So, during the mid-point, they need to have a glimpse of how it might all resolve. It should give the reader a very clear insight into the 'what's this really about?' question we asked earlier. What's important is that whatever crisis or enlightenment your character experiences here, it should point them towards the ending. They have to act. If they don't act, their life will be worse. They have experienced enough pain and they can no longer return to where they were at the start. It's the point of no return emotionally for them.

The mid-point is about a reversal of fortune, but not before the protagonist sees what the future could look like if they persist. You might see a superhero, post-montage, go on their first mission, and they might do something right, before it all goes wrong. That's the mid-point. The recognition that they can do something right, and that they're not where they need to be yet. Think of the mid-point as a break in the story, between the first half, which establishes what our protagonists want, and the second half where they establish what they need and act accordingly. Imagine, person A breaks up with person B and person B is traumatized, despondent, ruined. They may do everything possible to win person A back, thinking this is the route to happiness. But at the mid-point, person A and person B might reconcile, which is what person B wants, and person B might realize, in that moment, they're still unhappy. And the cause of their unhappiness wasn't actually breaking up with person A, it was something else, something deeper. The second half of the story, post mid-point, might be about the person trying to work out what makes them happy or why they aren't who they want to be when they're with person A. This is where, usually, you might want to expand the world of the story.

The Low Point: So the resolution has been glimpsed. There is motivation, but not so fast. You're not going to make it easy for your character to succeed. Because they're past the point of no return, and they're proactively seeking a resolution, they're going to get stuff wrong. You need to drive them to the low point, because it is only at their lowest ebb that they begin to change. When every path, bar the most difficult, has been closed off, a shift occurs. And my lord, if they go for the most difficult path, they'll fully self-actualize. It'll be painful. But self-actualization is painful! So, as with the mid-point, where you pointed towards a glimpse of a resolution, the low point is where you show them the mirror opposite of a good resolution: the worst possible resolution. That'll be the thing that makes them realize only the hardest path is the one that'll allow them to get through.

Low points bring about change because if a character acts, when the easiest path would have been inaction, they build character. Building character is a core driver of interest in the story. The half-unconscious boxer, who gets up before the count has ended, for one last grapple with the big bad dude. The hero who has had a building dropped on them, who pushes it off and goes to stop the bad guy getting away. The person who buys a ticket (and the only one left is a first-class one, non-refundable, to the Maldives), so they can chase the love of their life through an airport (in a pre-mobile phone world), so they can say, 'Stay. Please, just stay.' The guy who knows his friend has finished his bid for class president with any panache or sense of event, so dances badly to a Jamiroquai song so people know how much the election means to him. Low points are character-defining, not building. Because the virtue is inside the character all along, whether it's strength or bravery or an admission of undying love – it was always there. The character wasn't willing to admit it until they were on the brink of losing everything.

This is agonizing to witness and so we all shout, TELL HER HOW YOU FEEL.

Imagine a moment of truth when you find out someone from your past is not who they pretended to be, but is instead cold-hearted and selfish. Surely the easiest thing to do would be to put that skeleton back in the cupboard and get on with your life, because it's been so long? It may have destroyed you, but it's the truth, so you confront the offending party and tell them the devastating impact they have had on your life. This is your low point, the moment where the easiest thing to do would be to give up, or to go home, or to stay quiet. But no, if your character wants to become the person they're meant to be, they must act, even when all hope is lost. What could be more character-building than that?

These points, the attack, mid- and low, occur in most stories – whether subtle or in your face. Because these points give rise to action, and also propel our protagonist forward. The first is external: stirring them out of a metaphysical slumber. The second is internal: finding agency and acting because they have nothing left to lose. The third is the final push, a decision you make when all is lost.

Think of your story as having at least these three peaks of high drama. They are sequences to build up to and spend time in because it is where our characters are truly revealed.

*

You might be panicking, thinking I have none of these, or these don't feel relevant or this feels too intrusive to crowbar into what I'm planning to write. And I get that. These moments, the three big points of character development aren't necessarily about big fights or crashing buildings or grand gestures of love declaration. They are about finding what is important for your character. Sure, in a superhero world, the stakes are big enough for the building to fall down. Of course a boxer needs to be shown she can lose in order to fully understand what it means to win. Naturally, in a romantic comedy, you want the grand gesture to cut through all the misunderstandings, because, finally, the words that have needed to be said for the last few hours are finally said. But what might be right for your characters is something quieter: their low point is that they miss the train or they might not get the job they needed, or they might decide to leave the house for a change. Think of it in terms of what's truthful. It has to be truthful and important for the characters.

Story isn't about forcing these narrative peaks and troughs. Story is about recognizing what is driving a reader forward, what is keeping them turning the page. They're not always big moments. Sometimes a character can see a dad throw his baby in the air and catch her and they giggle together and that be enough for them to realize something about themselves. The way these moments manifest can be subtle, they're not always about ta-da, gotcha or pizzazz. And even if you're writing non-fiction, a personal essay or something else, remember that these story tricks can help propel things forward.

Writing Prompt
(2 hours)

This one is a hard one. Write down the plot of your story. You can have as many sides of paper as you want, but what I want you to do is consider writing the plot as a series of statements. This happens, and this happens, and this happens. Simple statements of plot. Each plot point is its own paragraph. I want you to think of the story in terms of BUT and BECAUSE. Start introducing BUT and BECAUSE into the action because these words help drive story. And drama. And an unfolding plot.

Michael goes to buy a pint of milk. BUT the shop is closed. BECAUSE the shop is closed, he has to walk for ten minutes. BUT he is accosted by an alien who has crash-landed. BECAUSE Michael is in a rush, he punches the alien. And so on.

The point of this exercise is to establish causality in your story. Cause and effect. Choice and consequence. The balance of external events and internal resolutions. And once you have this down, you might want to look at whether you have an attack point, a mid-point and a low point. And if not, what is driving the story forward. What is keeping the reader glued to the page?

Writing Prompt
(1 hour)

Write a short story about your morning. In this story, there is a breakfast you have been looking forward to for ages (if you're one of those strange people who thinks breakfast unimportant, use your imagination).

Except, the one ingredient that you need to make this breakfast perfect is missing/gone off (dealer's choice).

Write three versions of the story, with the discovery in Story 1 as the attack point, Story 2, the mid-point, and in Story 3, the low point.

You may make it as fantastical as you want, and have as many characters as you need. The purpose of this exercise is to use the same event to push different modes of storytelling and different parts of a character's arc.

What is a superhero origin story?

Superhero origin films are well-structured ways of understanding how we should look at character. They are formulaic and useful for understanding the character's journey. There are other ways to illustrate this, but sometimes taking apart a well-worn trope can show us how we can utilize structure. But also, how structure can help us do anything. It's about masking the formula in exciting, interesting characters doing unexpected things and seeking resolutions that'll mean the world for them.

Your story may not feel like a superhero origin story, but when you're first starting out and wanting to understand the mechanics, the following can help.

Imagine a person, an ordinary person. Let's call her Secret Identity. Secret Identity is far from where she wants to be in life. There is something in her self-image that keeps holding her back and preventing her from becoming the person she's meant to be. We establish who her friends and foes are, who her family is, and what she yearns for. This is the flow of her life, the way things currently are. Maybe she's disrespected in her job and no one can hear her or she's practically invisible in her school and no one notices her.

Establish what it is about her that needs to change. And think about how her story needs to start. And how the universe decides to intervene. The universe (or you as creator) can cosmically see that she is protecting that thing at the core of her, which means she hasn't yet become her fullest self. If she wants to achieve her big dream, if she wants to live her life to its potential, she has to do something about it. So the universe gets its cosmic hands dirty and intervenes. It knocks her off course. This is a point of attack, this is an inciting incident, this is external pressure – all the terms you may have heard screenwriters toss about.

However, in this case, Secret Identity is knocked off course and falls into a vat of radioactive waste, or is stung by a supernatural spider or gets an amulet containing powers (attack point anyone?). She is now externally strong. She hasn't worked out how to address her internal problems, her internal self-worth, her internal strength. Currently she is externally strong. Only. She has new powers, and that is destabilizing to her. She is knocked off course and confused about what this all means for the life she formerly knew. But that life does not exist anymore.

Destabilized, she tries to get back on course. Maybe she ignores her powers, maybe she uses them for something selfish, maybe she uses them preternaturally. Either way, by ignoring this new external strength, or using it to get what she wants, she is taking the easy way out. She isn't addressing her internal dysfunction yet, only using external powers. And the universe, in its cosmic wisdom, is wise to nonsense like that. And the thing is, when you're destabilized and you try to shortcut your way back to the well-trodden path of limiting yourself, you make things worse and you create a dilemma. (In the first issue featuring Spider-Man, Amazing Fantasy #15, when Peter Parker discovers his powers, he decides to use them to make his fortune, so he becomes a wrestler, getting paid to win matches. However, through his wrestling, he creates a chain reaction that results in the death of his dear uncle Ben. And he realizes that using these powers for personal gain is perhaps a bad thing. With great power comes great responsibility.)

And the dilemma concludes the first act. Secret Identity has now created the dilemma she is trapped in.

And this thrusts her into Act 2. The beginning of Act 2 is about understanding the limits and potential of her external strength. We see it impact on her life and we see her try to master her skills. She is being reactive to these new circumstances. She hasn't quite got a handle on things yet and she is not in control. All the while, we see the rise of the big bad villain she'll have to go toe-to-toe with a bunch of times over the course of the story.

At some point, once she has seen what her powers can do, we have the traditional montage of her running, jumping, climbing trees, punching things, and we see that she's getting better and better and more confident, and she's looking more like a hero. Maybe at the end of the montage, we reveal the suit for the first time, the thing we've been waiting for, and forty minutes have passed. But here she is, a hero, looking out over her territory, ready to save the day.

And then, we hit the most important part of her origin story: her first mission, usually signifying the mid-point.

Maybe she hears someone shouting, 'Save me!' and she heads over to see what's going on. Maybe she's in the right place at the right time. Maybe the big baddie is doing a minor bad somewhere nearby. So she starts the mission. And . . . wow, she has learned a lot in that three-minute montage. She is brilliant and fast and powerful, and all the external strength she has been building is on full display. But the thing about external strength is, it's a limited resource. It has a capacity. And in that mid-section, as she attempts to stop the heist or put an end to the fight, or chase the bad guys, she does something amazing – surprises herself. Even the bad guys are surprised. It is brave and spectacular and it is a culmination of a potential resolution for her. The moment she sees herself as a hero. She sees it. Wow. A resolution, an ending: she is a hero! Amazing! Yay! Go Secret Identity! Well, now she's known as Power Person. Go Power Person! Remember this culmination. Remember this moment of success and savour it because it is very short-lived.

Because in the next moment, a reversal of fortune (waaaait-a-minute, the mid-point?!) occurs, and she is right back to where she started. She is only externally strong, so a mistake that she makes, or an oversight, or a bit of ego means that she manages to fail at her mission and the bad people abscond with the goods. And maybe she's lying on the road, eating tarmac, banging her fists on the ground in frustration. Because, in this mid-point, she failed. And the failure has to have big repercussions for her. Maybe she failed, and the cops arrived on the scene and felt she meddled in police business and now they think she's a menace. Or maybe there is collateral damage and someone, an innocent bystander or passer-by, gets injured or worse.

She failed, but this is a critical moment. Because she may spend the next few scenes trying to return to normal, Power-Person suit thrown in the bin, what's the point, she messed up, what a failure. But that glimpse of resolution keeps niggling at her. Or she may be even more determined to get the bad guy.

Either way, she has the second half of the story to become the person she's meant to be. She has to switch up from reactive to her new surroundings, her destabilized self, to proactive. She knows now what she is capable of. And whether she is compelled to by a sense of justice, or the fact that she's being chased, she has to marry her internal strength with the external strength she spent the first half exploring. Now it's on.

So in the second half of Act 2, post-mid-point, we have an expanded universe – she is going to take down the big bad. The obstacles are around her, getting stronger, braver, trying to understand what it is that caused her to fail. And she will exhaust option after option, overcome obstacle after obstacle to reach her resolution. She's getting closer to that big baddie, closer to realizing her goal of being the superhero she was destined to be, the superhero she trained to be, the superhero that'll ease her demons and perhaps give her more self-worth rather than self-loathing.

But still, that resolution eludes her. Why?

In order to self-actualize and become the person she's meant to be, she has to summon up internal strength. So, as we head for the final showdown with her and the big bad, something dramatic is about to happen. She will fight, and fight, and move towards her resolution of being the best superhero that ever lived, finally worthy of the mantle of Power Person. But, alas, one more time, at a critical juncture, her fatal flaw, her weakness, the darkness that stalks her self-image causes her to lose. And lose big.

Maybe a building falls on her. Or she is beaten to within an inch of her life. Or the bad guy is too powerful.

All hope is lost. The easiest thing to do would be to lie down and give up, let the big bad win and lose your life. The stakes have never been higher. This is life or death. This is the end. Power Person has exhausted all her external strength. All that is left is Secret Identity. And Secret Identity could give up, or Secret Identity could harness that internal strength that has been lying dormant within her, clench her fists and stand up for one last go.

This is her low point. This is the moment she should give up. And yet, she finds it within herself to stand up and fight again. The weakness that has held her back her entire life. The self-doubt. The self-image. The thing that allowed her to be bullied by people lesser than her. That guilted her into desperate decisions to people-please. That meant she never knew who she was.

And yet, it is Secret Identity who stands up. Not Power Person. Because Power Person is nothing but a name and a mask. It's who is under the mask that counts. It's her inner courage and strength and power. That is the key.

So, in that moment, she self-actualizes. Internal strength and external strength combine. Resolve hardens. Confidence rises. She is now the person she is meant to be. She is the superhero, Power Person, not in name only. She is her true self. A hero to be reckoned with.

And so, this brings us into Act 3, the final showdown. She and the baddie tussle and fight and this time, the big bad is surprised – she is stronger, faster, more agile, more powerful than previously reckoned. She's Power Girl. She's Secret Identity, she is both, a whole of both, not a half of each! Go, Secret Identity, The Power Girl!

However, just because things are going well for her doesn't mean that the baddie is going to wave a white flag and accept defeat. No, no. They are going to keep going, and because they're big and they're bad, they've prepared for this. They have one more trick up their sleeve, probably a dirty one. And it's going to be surprising, and it's going to count as a story reversal. Because this one more trick is going to test our newly self-actualized hero. And it'll be hard. But they will win. And they will find their resolution.

The big baddie is defeated.

And that first culmination of a resolution we saw in the mid-point? Now it's a real thing. Power Person is now a force to be reckoned with.

This is their origin story. They're now ready for the second part of such a trilogy: rise and fall.

I know, I know, this is a very conventional structure. I say all this to help you peek under the hood of these films. They work in this way because . . . they work! This structure helps a character come of age and become the person they're meant to be. Sure, we can mess around with the order and the journey. Sure, we can ensure that this doesn't follow convention. Sure, our characters won't always fit this mould. But I wanted to show you why this structure works. Because it's so easy to look at blogs on the eight-point story arc of stasis, trigger, quest, obstacle, low point, climax, reversal, resolution. But unless you know *why* it works and how to apply it, and how it pushes character along a story arc, it's pretty meaningless.

I love these stories. They are about metamorphosis, they are about change, they are about becoming the person you're meant to be.

How do I ensure my protagonists feel like real people and not 'people in a story'?

Knowing the motivations of your characters, their vulnerabilities, their untapped strengths, the depths of their ego, the extent of their emotional baggage doesn't always make for a realistic character. They have to feel real in the world you've placed them in. They have to exist in their bodies. They have to have mannerisms and tics and ways of speaking and being in the moment. That's what we're going to focus on for the next few sections.

I once read a work of literary fiction that was acquired by a publishing house for a significant amount of money and heralded as startlingly original. And I read it and my response was: shrug. Mostly because the complex main character, the one we were all supposed to root for as he made it through a web of messed-up relationships, was one-dimensional. Every time he was nervous, he looked at the ground. Every time he was angry, he balled his fists in his jeans pocket. Every time he was sad, he disappeared to his cabin to play his guitar by himself. Is that it? The extent of his emotional range?

Zadie Smith said, in her lecture 'The I Who Is Not Me', that 'the hidden content of people's lives proves a very hard thing to discern; all we have to go on are these outward manifest signs, the way people speak, move, dress, treat each other . . . the way of things in reality.'

The interior should manifest in the character's exterior presentation from how they present themselves to strangers; how they act when no one is looking; how they perform under pressure; how they behave when they want something; how they dress to what they do with their hands and voice. All of these mannerisms cannot be random conflations you draw from the people around you. These characteristics have to mean something. They have to have been generated from something true to who they are in the moment and who they are to become.

For example, our mate Peter Parker, in the early issues of *Spider-Man*, wore round glasses and the sweater vest/white collared shirt combo stereotypical of the Sixties nerd. Although he was more powerful, strong and witty than any of his classmates, he hadn't realized this yet. He hadn't married his internal strength with his external one. And so, in his usual social setting, he was presented as a nerd, who liked science and taking photographs. An interesting theory I saw in the film *Kill Bill* was where the titular Bill (who needs to be killed) monologues about who was the real person, Clark Kent or Superman? Was Superman pretending to be Clark Kent or was Clark Kent acting as Superman? The theory he put forward was that Clark Kent was how the god-like Kal-El, the most powerful being on the planet, viewed the weakness of humans: mealy mouthed, earnest and bespectacled. Who was the real person? Were Superman and Clark Kent constructs? Who was Kal-El, really? Was Kal-El's truest identity a superhero who could leap tall buildings in a single bound, or was it the farm boy-turned-diligent journalist?

So with these two competing theories about superheroes in

your mind – yes, yes, Keshtastico is obsessed with comics – sometimes seeing things as starkly as light and dark, good and bad, can help us find our way to something subtler and more complex.

Visualize who your characters are. You can cut pictures out of magazines and use collage or you can write down notes, lists, inventories or even stories and anecdotes, or you can use something like an online pinboard website. Personally, I like a mixture of all three.

The only rule for these prompts is: don't make assumptions; make choices. Don't assume they wear jeans; decide on the style, the size, the cut, the wash of the denim and whether they tuck their shirt in or not.

Questions for developing your character's internal reality:

1. What makes your character happy? How does that happiness manifest? Tell me about a moment they felt truly happy.
2. What makes them anxious? What behaviours do they exhibit when anxious? What are the consequences of these behaviours, both for them and the people around them? Is there an original activating incident or childhood memory that has set them up to experience anxiety in this way?
3. How does your character react to pressure? How do they analyze a problem and go about solving it? What sort of team member are they? A strong, silent type, a true team player, or a managerial delegator? Give your character a problem with stakes that has no relation to your plot: for example, they are unexpectedly fired from their job and only have a small about of money to get them through the week. How do they go about getting on top of this issue?

    One of the things that makes a show like *Only Fools and Horses* so compelling is the drama around where the money is coming from. It's a real-world problem and a very relatable one: worry about paying bills, keeping a roof over a head, is absolutely something most people worry about month to month. If we're thinking about this in story terms, we equate money with security, and security leads to happiness. Obviously, in real life, it's not as simple as that. So, knowing how your characters may react in situations where they don't know where the money's coming from might give you an insight into how they deal with problems.

4. What do others think of your character? What would they say in conversation where someone says, 'Oh, I know your friend Dani . . .' How might they respond? What might they truthfully say about your character? Now, because this is an internal character-building exercise, let's pivot to this: how does our character think others see them? Because it's rare, we have the sufficient introspection to see ourselves as others might. How do our characters imagine the way people think about them? Build up a profile: what might this character think their parents say about them, their best friend, their significant other (past or present), their boss, their staff, their children? If their dog could talk . . . I'm joking. But in all seriousness, you can tell a lot about a person in fiction or scripts from how they treat animals. There's literally a screenwriting book called *Save the Cat!* that posits this as a big character trait. Will your bad-boy assassin getaway driver with nothing to lose swerve the getaway car to save a cat?

5. We all have that something we do or think or look up on the internet or sneak when no one is watching. And if we were found out, we'd feel a sense of shame. For me, it's constantly eating. Not out of hunger, but out of stress or boredom. I feel shame every time I eat an unnecessary

peanut butter sandwich at midnight so I can stay awake and watch season 6 of *Seinfeld*, a season I have gorged on many times since the mid-nineties. Why am I admitting this in a book? Now that I've drawn your attention to this habit, I feel such shame about it. What's that feeling for your character? If you're one of those people who don't think you do this, note next time what you're looking up on the internet on incognito mode when you can't sleep. This work is about digging into our characters' psyche, knowing what they're like at their most private and intimate.

6. What does your character wear? Make choices, from underwear to footwear to outerwear. Are brand names appropriate? Do they care about their appearance? How do we know? A red roll-neck jumper owned by their brother and handed down when his brother died. It still has spaghetti stains down the front from when his brother washed them in after their farewell dinner. This level of detail tells us a lot about someone, much more than that he wore something warm. Knowing someone likes to wear things with visible brands but buys knockoffs in charity shops in rich areas might say something about the facade they wish to present and the lengths to which they will go to achieve that. It also tells us about their biggest fears. Their shoes, their socks, their scent, that they only wear long sleeves, even in summer. It all tells you about them.

7. Tell us about their facial expressions. I say this as someone with limited facial expressions. I either look blank, sad, or smiley. Try to visualize what they look like when they're smiling, what that does to their face. When they listen, what do they do with their hands; their face? In fact, that's a good aside here: what kind of listener are they? Are they an active listener, present in the conversation, able to reflect

back to the speaker their thoughts and offer compassion and empathy before offering advice? Are they encouraging, giving the other space to speak but never offering anything of themselves other than an ear? Are they the type of person who isn't listening, instead they're waiting for their turn to speak, a very 'me now/me next' kinda person? Are they a 'just like me' sort of listener, who always has a story of how the same thing happened to them? If you're unsure of any of these, next time you're in a conversation, observe the people participating in it, and see if you can spot any of these tropes? Facial expressions, body expressions, how they view the world and their place in it, how they take up space or don't, how they act in conversation or don't, how they are in social situations or aren't, how they act when happy, sad, neutral, what that does to their face, their body? All of these things matter. Which is why, going back to the example earlier of the angry dude who balled his fists in his jeans, it doesn't work for me. It feels like a cheat, a shortcut. When actually the sum of a person, especially one experiencing a big emotion, like anger, is much more complex, much more wide-ranging than a balled fist. Keep an inventory of these characteristics. They may not make it onto the page, but if you can see what your characters look like, and visualize the specificity of their mannerisms, your writing of them will be more humane, accurate and realistic.

8. What do they eat and what do they drink? Do they care about food or is it fuel? Are they a fussy eater or only eat the finest things? Do they drink hot drinks or cold ones? If they have a fridge, what is the state of their fridge? Filled with fresh things or half-empty condiment bottles and gone-off milk? Their bedroom? Their bathroom? How

clean is it when we meet them? Generally? What is the ordinary of their life? How can you boil that down to its very essence?

9. Now take some time to think about:
    - their earliest memory;
    - their happiest moment;
    - the time they felt most like themselves;
    - the event that stunted their personal growth;
    - how they were in school;
    - how they are considered by colleagues.

    I'm making a lot of assumptions here because you might be writing historical fiction or something set elsewhere at another time. There are degrees to which these questions can help with world building. And if you're writing memoir, these can help bring characters to life.

10. Do they like surprises?

    You can tell a lot about a person from how they react to surprises. I don't like surprises personally. Mostly because my default is to assume it's going to be something bad. What does that say about me? Might I be considered a spontaneous type if I like surprises? Or someone who likes attention? It's a response to spontaneity, to events that aren't expected. So, does your main character like surprises?

    BOO!

    Do you?

What do my characters sound like?

One way to showcase character, story, tone and plot is to have your characters talk to each other. And we, the reader, the viewer, the active audience member, be immersed into the world by how it sounds. Dialogue lifts scenes out of long descriptive passages. It lifts characters out of inertia. It lifts the energy and the momentum on the page.

It's my favourite thing to write.

I love making characters talk. I like listening to what they say and don't say, what they talk about instead of the thing they need to talk about, how they make each other laugh, how they care for each other, how they understand each other, themselves, the world, all through dialogue.

Dialogue is hard to get right. It's also imperative you get it right. Dialogue should move the plot forward, tell us about the characters and feel true to how people actually talk, all at the same time, all without showing the reader we're doing any of these things.

Dialogue needs to contain action, exposition, story, backstory, feeling, drama, character and plot all at once.

Dialogue needs to also sound like it's spoken.

There is a story about the film set of the first *Star Wars* film, where Harrison Ford said to George Lucas about the script, 'You can type this shit, but you sure can't say it.' Which is to say, sometimes, what we write as speech on the page would sound preposterous said out loud. When characters talk fluidly in long flowing compound sentences, with big words and no pauses, as if everyone is sitting at their feet listening to them pontificate, is that how they sound? When characters say what they're thinking, is that how they sound?

Dialogue is meant to be spoken. It's meant to be a conversation. It's meant to ebb and flow, go back and forth, like a badminton rally. It's supposed to feel alive. It's supposed to be on its feet. It's supposed to be spoken by characters who are feeling things while in a space doing things.

Simple dialogue writing trick: Say the lines out loud. Feel how they sound. Do the lines sound like things people would say?

Another trick: Remember to have your characters move, pause, do things with their hands, think things before replying, get distracted by phones or whatever as they try to talk.

We'll get to how those of you writing about actual conversations might want to think about approaching dialogue, because remembering a conversation accurately, and within as objective a perspective as possible, is a hard, hard thing to do. But bear with me: we'll get there.

GOOD DIALOGUE: Should be written like it's spoken. So read it out aloud to yourself. Do the characters' voices feel distinctive? Can you tell them apart? Do they all sound like you? Are you using *you are* instead of *you're*? Is this the moment the character needs to say *you are*, not *you're* for emphasis? It needs to read like it's been said. So read it aloud to yourself. This isn't about giving your character a thick accent or dialect, but it may be a good place to recognize regional specificity, vocal tics and the manner of speaking. Maybe this is a character who asks themselves questions before they answer them. Am I in love with Sophia? Good question, I think I am. Are they the type of person who sits on the fence? Do I want to go to the pub? Could do, yeah. Let's hold fire. Are they the type of person who says exactly what they're thinking at all times? Uh-oh, how can we use that? Really think about the way people speak. A good thing to do is sit back in group situations and listen. In my friendship group, one of us needs to relate everything back to their personal experience, another is quiet unless there's a joke to be made. We have a contrarian and a romantic and I am called upon for the moral compass. We aren't always only occupying these roles, but often we default there. So listen to conversations around you and make notes of how people speak, and pull apart their conversational spaces.

Tip: Assign your friendship group roles in a conversation. Imagine who is the leader, who is the clown, who is the schemer, who is the nurturer. Then, once you've identified that, work out how they talk. Does the leader dictate the flow of conversation? Does the clown only ever crack jokes? Does the schemer always have a hack for everything? Does the nester offer everyone advice? And once you've identified their role and how it manifests, listen out for what is said and how it is said. What words do they use? Is the leader using clear, action-based instruction? Does the nester have a softer voice? Does the clown shrilly repeat the joke under the noise of conversation to the point where it has space to be heard? It's fun analyzing your pals. Or family. And once you spot the patterns, you'll learn loads about dialogue.

BAD DIALOGUE: Is exposition. It conveys information clunkily. Often information the characters already know. Just to ensure the reader is keeping up. 'Listen, Jonny, we have to get to the house before the serial killer does because he has our keys, from when you dropped them in the abandoned quarry.' You can do the same thing with, 'Hurry up, Jonny.'

Exposition is what we call the backstory, the social, political details of the time we need the reader to know, as well as the specific story, backstory and plot we need the readers to know to move forward. We've all seen those sci-fi films where someone has to explain how the world works to our hapless hero. Some exposition scenes are info-dumping, containing nuggets that'll come in handy later. Bear in mind these are the scenes that people put in so a detail can be used later on. Like someone might say, the bad guy has a weak left knee, and the audience will think, that's an odd detail for this plot involving mass destruction. But it's only so when the hero remembers the weak left knee at the point of highest tension, kicks it and saves the day that we, as the audience, feel glad we already knew about it. This is info-dumping. This is not trusting your audience enough to keep up. Obviously, when we are building up the worlds our stories exist in, there are details we need the reader to know. Like the political situation in Prague in the sixties, or how the gravity anti-matter machine has created a wormhole or how a certain piece of equipment works. We want our audience to keep up. But having characters explain the plot to each other in huge info-dumping monologues is bad writing, and it's bad dialogue.

Think of exposition as something you can show through actual action. This is what we mean by 'show; don't tell.' Don't tell me how the dream-scape architecture stuff in the film *Inception* works; show me. Often, this can mean using entertainment and action to give us crucial information. In terms of dialogue, keep it brief. Keep it pointed. And keep it relevant to the moment. Two characters who have worked together for years and have been on this case for five days might not need to review their reasons for staking out the husband's office during the stakeout. They know why they're on the stakeout. Trust the reader to know too.

GOOD DIALOGUE: Says what the characters are thinking without saying what they're *actually* thinking. Would a character say, 'I need you' in this moment? Or would they say, 'Can you get the next train?' What's not said is often the most interesting thing. What's said in the pauses, in the things we do instead of talking, the things we say instead of what we're thinking.

This is about using dialogue to give your characters opportunities to misunderstand each other (drama!) or talk about everything that's not the thing they should talk about (why solve the structural issue in our co-dependent relationship when I could eviscerate you for buying yet another coffee cup when there's a cupboard filled with coffee cups?). Dialogue is about putting us in real-life situations where what's said is often not far from the surface and arguments rarely start in a good-faith place. For example, a character might be on their way to the restaurant to propose to their partner. But because the bus is late, they're late. And they're always late, and their partner mentions this, which results in a tense argument about respecting each other's time as well as each other as people. Which pushes the proposal to later. But in this argument, we get an insight into their relationship and what is the most present obstacle to happiness in their way.

Tip: Write down an argument you've had recently with a loved one, or a boss (some of you may love your boss – I have never loved a boss, hence the distinction). Now write down what the argument was about. Now write out the dialogue of the argument where the thing that the argument is about is never said but never far from the surface. Now write down the dialogue of the argument where what's thought and felt is said unedited. Which of these conversations reads better? Which is more realistic? Which is more likely to be read and understood by a reader?

To illustrate this, look at this conversation:

Person 1: We must venture to the depths of the forest, for there we will find, once spoken by the wizard, Paul, a legend of epic proportions where the light and the love and the anxieties of the universe will coalesce into one energy source that we can harness to vanquish the evil foe.

Person 2: I know. I was standing right here the entire time he explained it to you. I have ears.

Now look at this:

Person 1: Hurry up, Jonny.
Person 2: Let me finish my breakfast.
Person 1: No.

BAD DIALOGUE: Reminds readers of relationships unnecessarily. 'Bob, you're my husband, you should know where the coffee pot is.' 'Barbara, as my sister, you need to phone Mum.' Yeuch.

This is one of my least favourite things a lot of sitcoms. *Friends* was the worst culprit. Monica and Ross had to constantly remind each other they were brother and sister, for comedic effect. It was excruciating, and worrying if it had been in the real world. You see it a lot. People reminding people they're best friends. People reminding people they've known each other for years. People reminding people that they've not been going out for a long time.

'Paul, we've been best friends since we were four. How could you say that about me?'

'Paul, I've known you my whole life. You're scared right now.'

'Paul, we've only been together for two weeks, so this proposal feels rushed.'

Now, however much we may do this in real life, and we don't actually do it often, the reality is, you're doing this to remind the reader. Don't. Stop. You need to treat your reader better. They are smart, you know! Treat them as such.

GOOD DIALOGUE: Is conflict! Drama! Arguments! Questions unanswered! Emotions left unsaid! Details purposefully omitted! This is what will drive your plot forward.

Dialogue is a construct. Dialogue is the way we communicate in real life. But as we've said above, it's about conveying so much, from character to tone to setting to plot to story. So the way we use it in our stories is a construct. It's a storytelling technique masked as the way of things in reality. Now we want it to sound as real as possible. But in real life we don't always have conversations that matter. A lot of small talk. A lot of grunts. A lot of dead ends. Stories don't need to be like that. Conversations matter. What we omit and what we don't matters. For example, if we had the boy and the girl go on the date, we may skip over a bunch of things before slowing down the moment that matters.

They spoke about their jobs; her making him laugh with impressions of her boss; him trying his best to make her think what he did was important when actually, it wasn't, and he knew it, no matter how many times he tried to convince everyone, especially himself. They discussed their favourite cocktails, best London nights out. After a while, Paul leant across the table and offered his hands to her.

'I've never met someone like you,' he said. 'I feel like I've known you my whole life.'

Hot diggedy, guys, now we're cooking. We know that this is a significant moment because we've slowed it down and given it weight. We know that his saying this changes everything that happens next. It's important. Dialogue is driving us forward here.

I used to think that the first five minutes of the film *Reservoir Dogs* were so pointless, such an ego-trip for the writer-director, Quentin Tarantino. Because it's all the bank robbers, sitting in a diner, arguing about tipping waitresses and Madonna records. I had no idea what bearing it had on what came next. It seemed to be a case of Tarantino shoving his favourite pet theories into the film. (We'll get to that next.) But actually, on reflection, I realized how clever it was to set a scene before the ensuing chaos where we get to see these characters operating in a safe environment with no stress. And actually, everything each person said told us everything we needed to know about their character. Through their attitudes to tipping wait-staff and their differing attitudes to Madonna, we see the hierarchy of the group established: who has what role in the group, who is high status, who is low status, who has power, who wants power and so on. The moment we cut to the warehouse and everyone is operating at a high level of stress, we will understand their roles because of this opening scene. This is all character set-up and done in such an entertaining way that it actually brings levity to the screen before everything goes very wrong – before, as the old *Bad Boys II* adage goes, '[redacted swear word] gets very real'.

BAD DIALOGUE: Is you stating your opinion, in the characters' voices, about various social and political and religious themes and ideas. It's padding, it's pontificating, and it's not readable or believable. My initial reaction to the opening of *Reservoir Dogs* was that it was a meaningless excuse to include a fun pet theory about 'Like a Virgin'. It took me a second to realize that actually it served a purpose in terms of character. If your characters are going to exchange long emails about their lives, sure you might use these as an opportunity to tell us about their worldview, but don't use it to pontificate on the world like your story is a series of tweets about a breaking news story. I say this as someone who is guilty of having done this in the past.

In one of my novels, I wanted to talk about some of the post-colonial literature I was reading and also put it into some naturalistic conversation between characters, but I couldn't exactly have characters cite Edward Said and Frantz Fanon to each other. That wouldn't work. One of the characters was a stand-up comedian who was learning more about himself and his place in the world. He was reacting to conversations he was having with people around him and racist incidents within his industry. I worked out that the best way to show his growth would be to put him in a situation where he got to tell some stand-up about colonialism, and then undercut it with a big joke that escalates the situation and also makes him realize how much further he has to go. So I got to put a pet theory, or some thoughts spinning out of reading I was doing, into the mouth of a character in a way that drove them forward and undercut it with some tension so it never settles in as a theory.

GOOD DIALOGUE: I don't want to be alone tonight.

BAD DIALOGUE: Please don't leave me. I'm so scared of being alone. It's my biggest fear.

Putting these two side by side, I think we can see that the first one is definitely good drama. The subtext is clear. It's punchy; it reads like it could be said; it reads like there are more things underneath the surface. The second one, on the other hand, feels melodramatic. It's not punctuated in the way someone might talk, and it pulls us into characters telling each other everything. Where do you go in the first one and where do you go in the second one? They're both saying the same thing. But one offers opportunity for complex, nuanced drama and the other pulls us into a shouty argument.

GOOD DIALOGUE: Has a rhythm. It's different from real life. It's conveying so many things. Plot and story and tone and character and what is left unsaid and said instead. So, in order for it to do all this work, it needs to be rhythmic. Like poetry. If you watch a Coen Brothers film or read a Kevin Barry short story aloud – or Sally Rooney, Brandon Taylor, Zadie Smith or any writers incredible at dialogue – you'll quickly see what I'm talking about. It's like poetry. Stops and starts create a rhythm. The lengths of sentences create a rhythm. You're not writing out full sentences, filled with compounds and without contractions. You're trying to make it sound like it's spoken.

Rhythm is a hard thing to convey. If you're wondering how on earth to start, think about how Shakespeare uses dialogue. Writing in iambic pentameter, speech goes ta-tum, ta-tum, ta-tum, ta-tum, ta-tum. It's a line of verse with five metrical 'feet', each consisting of one short (or unstressed) syllable followed by one long (or stressed) syllable, for example: *Two households, both alike in dignity.*

If you want to start experimenting with rhythm, have your characters talk in this short, unstressed syllable then long, stressed syllable pattern and see whether you can create a rhythm.

Person A: Would you like to go with me to the pub?
Person B: Yes please, darling. Never would I say no.

I know I'm cheating here a little because actual iambic pentameter requires a short percussive syllable followed by a long languid one. Instead, I opted for ten syllables. But you can see a rhythm forming.

Another way of forming rhythm through dialogue is to create call and response. Throw out a question, get an answer. Throw out a command, get an answer. Or using repeated phrases or tics as your chorus focal point. So maybe a character says 'yes indeed' no matter what is said to them. The trick, as I said, is to get it on the page, and then read it aloud.

Put in the pauses and the ellipses to show thoughts dangling or tailing off. Put in the stuttering, the stop-start, the yeah, quite and uh-huh. Work them into the rhythm.

BAD DIALOGUE: Is non-existent dialogue. If you find yourself summarizing the plot and moving your characters through scenes and reporting their interactions and instead telling us what they're thinking and how they get in and out of situations without rooting us in the moment, then you are not writing bad dialogue. You're writing bad prose. Fiction is a sequence of moments. Fiction is being in the moment of what's being narrated or what's being experienced. Now, you may want to summarize non-essential parts of a character's life. You might even find yourself skipping over them entirely. But if you want these moments to resonate, slow down and let us exist within them.

For those of you writing non-fiction, the process is similar. You might be reporting conversations or trying to figure out the essence of an exchange.

Now the thing to remember is, if you are recalling something that's happened to you, you won't remember it in any way other than from your own perspective. If I said to you now, 'My god I'm bored.' You might interpret it as 'you are boring me'. Whereas we might be sitting in silence at a train-station cafe nursing coffees waiting for our train. We bring different things to conversation and we ascribe different meanings to what others say.

So, with that in mind, it's important you think about the emotional truth of what you're trying to convey and the narrative lens through which your reader experiences the conversation. Be true to the narrator, to what they convey, what they glean, what they hear. Be true to the essence of what's said, but don't think too much about getting it down word for word. Don't offer us a transcription. Personal essays and memoir are imperfect by nature because we choose the narrative lens through which they're told and most of us rarely remember a conversation as it happened. The only thing we can do is retain the emotional truth of the narrator in how we use dialogue. We may not have pages of half-remembered conversation. But we can construct moments of drama and ensure that what's on the page sounds like the people we are trying to capture. Here's where all the character work we have done so far will come in handy. Because you'll already be thinking about these people as characters. You will have done the work on what they sound like. If they told this story from their perspective, they would tell it differently. You have to be okay with that. And they have to be okay with the truth you're telling, that it is yours. Other than that, there is not much else you can do. You might lose all the excess fat of a conversation to distil it down to its barest bones. You keep it brief. You might use it for impact. What you cannot do is try to capture any conversations as they happened to you. That way is impossible. You won't manage it.

So stick to the emotional truth. That's all you can do.

Writing Prompt: Things Unsaid
(1 hour)

Write a scene (max two pages) between two people. A wants to tell B 'I love you'. B wants to end things with A. Think about what they would actually say and how they would say it. What are they doing? What actions mask speech? What is the text? What is the subtext? What is left unsaid? Do they both get to say what's on their mind? Only one of them? Create conflict for them. Drama. Just don't let them say how they feel!

Writing Prompt: Script
(1 hour)

Think of a conversation you had recently, a significant one, one where you told someone something or you found out something and it changed the way you see things.

Now try to record it as it happened from your perspective.

Write it as a script. Add in pauses and action and movement as required. But distil it down to what's said and what's not.

Who do I know?

Stories are about people. And people need other people to bounce off, either positively or negatively. Stories need a cast of characters in order to move forward. Where would Dorothy be in the Land of Oz without her pals? She's the main character, but she finds three friends to help her navigate the world, and an antagonist in the Wicked Witch. More often than not, the main character in our story isn't operating in isolation. They are surrounded by people: friends, foes, family (who might be both friend and foe), advisers, mentors, tricksters, dependants. The trick you have to play as the puppet master is to ensure that your character is surrounded by people who will help or hinder them thematically on their journey.

These other characters add so much to our stories. They give our main character energy and purpose. They help build the world we're trying to establish. They point to other stories within that world.

We're going to talk about building the cast of characters in our story, and ensure they are servicing this story, not their own, while at the same time appearing on the page as fully formed people.

Here lies the tension of the cast of characters. They have to feel like they have lives of their own, stories of their own, troubles and victories of their own. If we followed them over the course of the day, they wouldn't be sitting in an isolation booth waiting to interact with our main character. No, we could imagine them at work or at home living a fulfilled life with a story of their own. When they leave the scene, when they're off camera as it were, they have their own life to lead.

But also, they have to be thematically linked to our main character in some way.

Take the film *Shaun of the Dead* again. The central premise is that Shaun needs to grow up. He's in a dead-end job and he does it hungover every day because he spends night after night with his best friend and his fed-up girlfriend in their local pub: his safe place, his citadel. Then a zombie apocalypse happens. Before we get there, though, let's think about his best friend, Ed. If Shaun needs to grow up, leave the dead-end job and consider his girlfriend's needs over his desire to be a barfly at the Winchester pub, then he has to be pulled in different directions. Ed represents to him a desire to maintain the status quo. But the status quo isn't doing anything for him anymore. He needs to grow up.

Meanwhile, Shaun and Ed's flatmate, Pete, is a smarmy go-getter who has his life together; someone with a proper job and life who owns the house they all live in. He represents the path Shaun should choose if he is to get Liz, his girlfriend, back. Liz wants him to be more Pete than Ed – even though the Ed version of him is the one she fell in love with. Now, all these characters are people in their own right, but they all represent a vision of Shaun's future. Each one will force him to choose. His mother babies him, which is why he hasn't grown up. His stepfather cares for him in an aggressive way to push him to be better, which makes Shaun in turn push his stepfather away. Liz has pretentious friends. And so, when the zombies come, they force Shaun to not only save everyone he knows, but also to save himself, by growing up.

And then, during the daring rescue, we meet Liz's friend Dianne and her boyfriend David, and we see that perhaps the way Shaun has idealized Liz isn't quite right. Because her friends are horrible, venal, vain, pretentious. They represent to him the worst parts of her in the same way Ed represents, to her, the worst parts of Shaun. Then we meet Shaun's mother and stepfather, and we understand why he has refused to grow up. Because his sweet mother coddles him and he responds to this by acting like a little boy. And his stepfather, while stern, wants the best for him, like Pete. Everyone fits perfectly into this cast of characters. They are all performing an important role in the story. They all matter to Shaun and his journey to hero later on. And they all feel fleshed out enough to be their own person.

I use this example as a perfect way of illustrating that groups of characters should fit together in some way, even if they are antagonists to each other. There is a symbolism in their relationship that we have to strive towards. It's not enough to plonk a character who's a bit like me and a character who's a bit like you on the page. We have to move them around a universe we have constructed for our readers, as we question the big things at the heart of what it means to be human, or some other vague notion on the meaning of art. In order to do that, we have to imbue each of our characters with purpose, drive, personality and their own story to tell, if given half the opportunity.

Even if you're writing a personal essay, you might want to think about who the cast of characters is. Who will show you the story you are trying to tell? Like, if you were writing a personal story about a family trip to the seaside, you might want to include uncles and aunts who were there, but focus on the mother and father. It's about establishing how the aunts, and which supporting cast members, are going to be useful in that instance.

As in real life as in story, we all perform roles.

I heard the comedy writer Mitch Hurwitz talking on a podcast about the classic construction of comedic families and their basis in the commedia dell'arte structure, an early Italian theatre form. Now while he said this with a particular focus on sitcom, it's definitely worth considering it in the wider scope of characters in stories in general.

He said that the classic sitcom family (and yes, this does rely on traditional gender roles) is the matriarch, the patriarch, the craftsman and the clown. See the breakdown below. And yes, I will illustrate them with extreme sitcom examples before we work out how they can be useful to our stories.

The matriarch is the nester. Everything revolves around their concept of home. They create a comfortable space for the rest of our cast to be themselves in. They run the safe haven. Think Monica in *Friends*. Think Jerry in *Seinfeld*. Specifically and obviously, the action all largely took place in their apartments. The action always led there and revelations took place there. There George could be his worst, Kramer his most selfish and Elaine her least empathetic. Monica cooked and cleaned for her found family; she was the matriarch. Meanwhile, Joey plotted ways to get with girls and Chandler was the architect of his own disaster. Rachel, well, it might have been her first job, but she was the ambitious career go-getter. Neither Ross nor Phoebe technically live in the building so are outsiders to the home space.

The patriarch is the provider. The patriarch holds down the stable job; they are dependable and they bring home the bacon. They are, in theory, the go-getter. They may prioritize their career and ambitions above the needs of the home. They are often selfish and entitled. Providing means they can allow themselves bad behaviour. Think of all those dads in sitcoms who are schlubby and hard-working but then spend most of their episodes trying everything they can to get away from their lovely wife and cute kids and golf or get blasted with their mates. Think of Elaine in *Seinfeld*. For a large part of its nine-season run, she is the one with the great job. She is rarely out of work, even if she's working for the fickle Mr Pitt. She has ambition, which drives the patriarch.

The craftsman is the schemer, the agent of chaos, the person who always has a shortcut to what they want. Usually in sitcom, it's money, or a sexual partner. They can never do things simply. Their plans are unnecessarily outlandish, ambitious and complicated. Their plans will ultimately fail. They won't be deterred. They have a million more plans. The craftsman is the person who often drives our main character, either the matriarch or patriarch, to exhibit their worst behaviours. At best, they are manipulative and charming. At worst, they are chaotic. They give stories structure and an architecture to operate within. Usually, in a story, the patriarch or matriarch will issue a desire and the craftsman will offer a solution. The solution will be bonkers and bound to fail. Or the craftsman will have a scheme and suck our cast into it so they are complicit in the chaos. Kramer in *Seinfeld*. Nuff said.

The clown is, sadly, the butt of the joke. They reflect the worst parts of us. They are not afraid to tell the truth, be their worst, be down on their luck, because they are the butt of the joke. The clown should never get what he wants and the reason should always be because the clown is the clown. They have no option but to remain the same in sitcom. Any attempt at growth should make their situation worse. Any attempt to do the right thing should blow up in their face. Any attempt to seek pleasure should be undercut by the reality. They are Icarus, flying too close to the sun. With hilarious rather than tragic consequences. This is George in *Seinfeld*, Chandler in *Friends*, Woody in *Cheers*, Pierce in *Community*.

*

So this is all great, but how do we work it into our stories? Well, think of these roles: the matriarch, the patriarch, the craftsman and the clown. Do they work with what you have? Or the nester, the provider, the schemer and the funny, sad one? How about these?

If this construction isn't obviously working for you, then try to think of your characters in terms of what they provide to the group. Give them roles. What function do they perform in the core of a group? Give it a go.

Once you've established what roles they perform, see if you can shape them into these specific archetypes.

The importance here is ensuring that everyone has a role to play in the story. If you haven't thought about your cast of characters, now is definitely the time. I've found that personal essays can stay too interior if you don't think of characters to lift it into action. Sure the interior is important, but as well as providing a structure for the character at the heart of the essay, the cast of characters widens the universe, ensures that we are always speaking to the wider world.

In terms of fiction, the cast of characters gives us a chance not for chaos and drama and conflict, but also for support.

Sometimes this extra work may feel extra. But you can use things like flashbacks to establish this wider world. They give our protagonists a structure to operate within. Obviously if you write, as I once did, a story about a spear fisher on a dive trying to catch something and feeling like the rest of their life was so out of control that they needed this moment of focus, it's okay to lean into the solitude. Some stories don't need a cast of characters. A loner might remain a loner. An interior story might remain interior. But give yourself opportunities to show readers more of the world.

Writing Prompt
(1 hour)

Take your cast of characters and have them perform a bank heist. Give them a clear want, a clear reason to do the heist, one that fits with what you know of them. Give each roles within the heist, allow them to lean into their darkest, basest instincts and propensity to do awful things. Because a heist is a stressful situation, it will give you a chance to see how your characters act and react under duress.

   Bonus points if the characters you choose are your family or friends. It'll be interesting to see what insight this situation gives you about the people around you!

   Have fun! This is a fun exercise! It's fiction, so no holds barred. Just remember to be as truthful as possible to who your cast is.

Who is telling this story and how are they telling it?

One big choice we have to make about our stories, aside from who the characters are, is how they are telling the story. Are we up close and personal, witnessing the story in the moment, or are we reflecting back? Who is the narrator and what is their lens?

Let's talk about perspective in the simplest terms we can.

Who is telling this story? Why them? Why them *now*? All of this is down to you as the writer. You know what you like to read and which voice will tell your story best. It's important to be consistent. At no point do you want your reader to lose confidence in you. The easiest way to lose a reader's trust is to fail to be purposeful in your decisions. Purposeful and consistent. For example, if you have multiple narrators and one voice is in first person present tense, another is in the past and another is third person, and so on, the reader is going to find it jarring, unless you make it clear why you're doing it the way you are. If you jump around the viewpoints of different narrators in the same chapter, your reader will lose track of what's going on to who, and by whom. There are many ways to write a novel, many voices, many reasons to use one over the other.

When I say 'perspective', it's often about how the story is being told. Is it set now; is the narrator the protagonist; is it close up to their interior or distant and all-seeing? These choices all have their pros and cons. Some writers prefer to not write the 'I' narrator; other writers only write the 'I' narrator. Some use different voices for each story, depending on what they wish to achieve; other instances, one might have no choice other than the 'I' or the omniscient narrator. Especially if you're writing something real. Let's go through some of the basic ones and some of their advantages and disadvantages so you can make informed choices about what works better for your voice and for your story.

First-person, present: I am narrating this novel as it happens to me right now. Everything that happens is stuff I experience or is told to me; all the information I possess or discover, the reader possesses or discovers alongside me. This is an immersive style. It allows the reader to experience your story as it happens. It is very 'in the moment'. There is no reflection unless we put pauses into the text. It can fully submerge the reader into the world and allow them to see the world as the protagonist experiences it. One of the disadvantages of this style is that the narrator, the person in the present tense, can only possess information as it is relayed to them. This can sometimes mean that the plot can only be experienced by the main protagonist as it happens to them. Explaining things gets a little trickier. But you get to immerse yourself in the delicious interior of a protagonist and have fun seeing the world through their eyes.

Can you think of a story you like that used this technique? Make a short list of all the things you enjoyed and perhaps didn't enjoy about this style of narration.

First-person, past: This is my story. I remember when this important thing happened to me years ago, and it's the reason I am who I am now. I have the benefit of hindsight. I have the benefit of experience, of knowing better. I have comparisons to draw between now and then, but most of the action takes place then. This is where a person might be choosing a fixed point now to reflect on something in their past. It may be a near past, in that it happened minutes ago, hours ago, days ago. But the fixed point is useful and important. You may be doing that thing of starting somewhere down the line of the story and getting to a moment of tension and then saying, ooop, record scratch, you may be wondering how I ended up here, and then using this style of narration to bring us back up to date. You may be years later reflecting on something in your past and how it has made you end up where you are currently. Questions to ask yourself with this technique are: what is the purpose of the reflection? What will it give the protagonist?

Can you think of a story you like that used this technique? Make a short list of all the things you enjoyed and perhaps didn't enjoy about this style of narration.

Third-person, close: She knew this was a good technique. Because while it was in a distanced third-person, she could still delve into her character's head. She was careful to not dip into the heads and viewpoints of others. She felt good about this. This is where we allow ourselves to have a bit of distance from our character but still jump into their head. The third-person narration gives us a bird's-eye view of the world, but it allows us to get close to how the characters might be feeling. We can jump in and out of their heads. The trick here is to not have too many perspectives to jump in and out of, as it can be confusing to the reader as to who the main focus of the story is. Having a way of marking out the differences in perspective is important for a multi-person narrative. You might have each chapter or section marked out with the name of the perspective you are jumping into. You might need to jump into different sections where you are clearly demarcating whose section it is. This allows you to show more of the world and show things happening simultaneously. It also gives you enough of the protagonist's interior to give us an insight into their world. However, you cannot over-deploy this in your narration.

Can you think of a book you like that used this technique? Make a short list of all the things you enjoyed and perhaps didn't enjoy about this style of narration.

Third-person, distant: It was a style he had grown up reading. He wrote relentlessly, stopping only to drink water and text his mum. The world knew about him only what was projected. And because he didn't say much, all the intention was in his action, or lack of it. The advantage here was authorial omniscience.

This is where we might want to show everything through action and give the reader enough space to see between the lines. Use what is said and how to understand subtext. The world is built through an objective, all-seeing eye. However, the all-seeing eye will have a gaze of its own. There is nothing objective in a narrative lens. It comes with the author's preconceptions of a world. What an author chooses to show is important. What an author deems important to discuss is important. We all have our biases and the omniscient narrator will come with its own biases. For example, I will see the world differently from you and as I build it up in my story, I may delve into different things about it. I may focus on certain types of people from certain backgrounds. I may notice different things to you when I describe the place, the time, the people who occupy the time and place. I may have preconceptions about their socio-economic status. I may have my own lived experience that will influence how my characters relate to the world.

Omniscience is a construct, and it's important to acknowledge that omniscience is biased by the author. We don't, any of us, have an all-seeing eye. And also, we, as the writer, choose what we show our readers and how we show it to them.

There are obvious advantages and disadvantages to this style, but it's important to recognize that it cannot ever truly be objective. So with our omniscience, what do we see? And how much of our authorial worldview do we leave on the page? How much can we ever write ourselves out of the worlds we build in our stories?

Can you think of a book you like that used this technique? Make a short list of all the things you enjoyed and perhaps didn't enjoy about this style of narration.

There are different viewpoints on offer, obviously. But you have to pick one and stick to it. It'll give you consistency in the narrative voice and help you make decisions about tone. There are advantages to each. I like the first-person present tense as a writer, because it puts my work on its feet, immerses the reader in the moment of the prose. Other writers employ other viewpoints. I guess the main thing is: make that decision and stick to it.

So I ask you again. Who is telling this story? Why them? Why them now?

Other techniques include the second-person narrator, using 'you' to address the reader directly. This is used to perfection in the non-fiction book *In The End, It Was All About Love* by Musa Okwonga and the novel *Open Water* by Caleb Azumah Nelson. Both different books using the same narrative technique to invite you in.

'You look at the train timetable and wait for the train. You're sad today. She texted you earlier saying she wasn't coming back.'

This is an arresting style, directly engaging the reader and pulling them into the narration, making them feel like they are part of it. It becomes our every story in that instance and can give us an immersive style that sometimes invites us to occupy someone else's viewpoint.

Other stories have used the collective 'we' to tell the story of different communities. Excellent examples of this are *This Brutal House* by Niven Govinden and *The Buddha in the Attic* by Julie Otsuka.

These have a cumulative effect of making the reader feel like they are part of a wider community and that the collective experience is a specific one and a universal one. It can be hard to sustain, but novels like Joshua Ferris's *Then We Came to the End* use this collective narration, without a single protagonist to tell the human story of how a company came to its end.

Choosing a narrative lens for your story can be an overwhelming decision and sometimes your first attempt might not be the right one. So don't be afraid to try different versions to see which fits you best.

Writing Prompt: Four Viewpoints

Have a go at writing about a typical morning for your character using one of the four narrative viewpoints suggested above. Make sure you include an interaction with another person in this scene you're writing, and perhaps some dialogue. These will help. If it's the same few lines of dialogue, you can see how each sits in each of those viewpoints. Really think about the differences between each and the opportunities and disadvantages you're given. Write about 500 words for each. Just to try it. You'll find one more natural than the others. Why is this?

How do I write about people I know?

Whether we're writing fiction or memoir, life writing or something entirely made-up, we will find ourselves drawing from our greatest resource: the people around us. And this can cause complications.

To tell you a story to hammer it home: the last conversation I had with my mother before she died was her upset at me for the depiction of the mother in my first novel. Because the main character was close to me, the natural assumption for her was that the mother, the overbearing source of anger and hilarity, was her. It wasn't. I had drawn from her and other people around me. And I'd pooled them together to create an entirely fictional comedic character.

I was stung by her words, embarrassed and defensive. And I didn't have time to convince her otherwise, because I brooded on our argument the rest of the day, and she died that night. Leaving what I wanted to say to her unsaid: that I loved her and that any portrayal in that book was one of love, and maybe she was seeing herself in that character for reasons nothing to do with me. I realize now the last bit is probably the bit that should remain unsaid. Otherwise it comes off as, 'stop projecting, dude,' which doesn't help.

So, there are some things to think about when it comes to drawing from real life.

No reader wants you to make proclamations about a person in your story. Bad writing is often about not trusting your reader and assigning labels to people and things. To call your characters evil, deviant, perverse, toxic or any other label is to undermine the work the prose is doing. There's that age-old adage, 'show; don't tell'. And it applies here. Don't tell me the character is evil. Show me through their actions. If you're writing non-fiction, be clear that it is your perspective. If you're writing fiction, be clear that it's not authorial voice passing judgement, but a character trait. Stick to the emotional truth of characters. Sure, it's a great shorthand to use elements of someone in your real life, but that can sometimes lead to a surface presentation of someone.

Think about it like this: the people in our lives, the ones who are positive and negative, exist. Their actions, be they positive or negative, whether they affect people positively or negatively, have consequences. The moment they arrive on the page is the moment you need to present them as human. I'm not saying you need to understand the reasons for their negative influence. Like, if you're writing about a Nazi, make them a Nazi; we don't need their Nazi origin story. But what you want to do is present them as complex. No one wants a simplistic character, good or bad. In short, use the prose to give us a portrayal of a character with no easy answers; leave those to the reader to define. Trust them to get what you're conveying by trusting your prose.

An easy way to address potential pitfalls of putting characteristics of people you know in fiction is to take the essence of the person and clearly attribute physical features to the character that are different from what they actually look like. You'll be surprised how few people spot versions of themselves in books. Especially if they are now blonde when they were auburn-haired, for example.

If you're taking a story you've heard in real life, maybe one that made you laugh or even one that shocked you, I'd change the story. You can boil down what shocked you or made you laugh down to the bare bones of comedy or tragedy. Also, have you ever tried to retell an anecdote someone else told you, and found yourself struggling to convey it in the same way? Imagine that, but putting into prose a fun night out you and your mates had. Is there something else you can do? If all else fails, get permission. If you can't get permission, ask yourself what this story will add.

If you are telling someone else's story, ask them. Fictionalize it as much as you can. Strip it down to the simple truth. See what details can be changed. See what things can protect that person. Mainly, a great story we hear doesn't always make for good prose. Stress-test this. Do you need it?

Where you don't know the facts, the ins and outs, the truth, be transparent about any speculation. Be clear, in non-fiction, that you're making assumptions or guesses; be honest. If it's fiction, well, fiction is your friend. Use this as an opportunity to further fictionalize, dig even deeper.

Prose is not the place to settle scores or get even. Do that over text or email if you need to.

Remember: you are a writer and the writing deserves the best you can give it. Bear that in mind as you pull from real life. And if all else fails, here is your line:

For fiction: 'It's all fiction. I can't be held responsible for what my readers project onto the text.'

For non-fiction: 'I told the truth as truthfully as it appeared to me. I'm sorry that this doesn't match with your truth. But what is truth? Can it ever be absolute? How about you tell me your truth.'

If either of these fail, try this: 'Wow, look, over there, an asteroid is hurtling to earth at great speed and the only people who can save us are a rag-tag group of industrial drillers,' then hide.

Now you know the pitfalls of drawing from real life, think of the advantages.

Looking at the people around you can give you a level of authenticity you can't make up. Observing how people are in public, how they present themselves, how they talk, stand, sit, eat, take up space in a group, laugh, cry – all these things need a level of authenticity. Taking note of them can give you actions for your characters, to bring them to life. Also, we are able to observe how people are in certain relationships and what those relationships might say about them.

Tune yourself into other people's voices. Listen to what they say, how they say it and what they don't say. Listen for their stumbles, verbal tics, interesting catchphrases. Make note of them.

Now observe how they dress. What do they wear? How often do they wear it? Is it a particular colour or a style? Is it always something new or always the same haggard cardigan?

I remember a friend saying of someone, 'He always wears exactly the right thing.' Which I thought was a brilliantly telling way of describing someone. She also said of me, 'You always know what colour pants Nikesh is wearing,' which was again brutal. I know what she was saying was, there's a performance in how I dress. But hey, rap fans have a dress code.

Once we have our characters' speech and their dress down, start thinking of their face. Observe them when they listen, when they look at their phone, when they type a message, when they tell you a story. What do their hands do, their face? What do they fiddle with?

Documenting all these things brings our characters to life. The thing is, we are surrounded by people, whether it's ones we live with, or ones we observe out and about. Even if we see people on television, what might we learn from people who are on reality shows? How do they act?

Often, these details won't make it onto the page, but they can help you visualize exactly who the people are when you're writing them. They come to life.

So, do it, but do it sensitively. And if you're writing fiction, use these real-life things to help you fictionalize. And if you're writing real people, make sure it's your perspective, and it's emotionally true and it ain't a cheap shot.

Or you'll end up like me and my mum.

And no one wants that.

Writing Prompt
(1 hour)

Think of someone in your life. Describe a typical morning for them. Write it in the first person. See the world through their eyes. Give your description flavour, right down to their mannerisms, what they do, say, eat, feel, don't say, how they move, what they wear. Push yourself to do an honourable depiction of someone else.

How do I make people complex?

Remember the light with the dark and the dark with the light. A dark and tortured character needs a sense of humour. A light and lovely character needs a dark side. We are all light and shade. We all contain multitudes. We find humour in the saddest of times and we can find the kernel of tragedy in the jokes that we tell.

Don't be afraid to push for both.

Surprise us with your characters. Have them make decisions one might not expect of them. Don't underestimate the power of the reader feeling a sense of superiority because they would never in a million years do that. How many times have you felt frustration at the character you love dating the wrong person, or the hunted character running up the stairs instead of out of the house? That superiority? That's an invested audience member being kept guessing.

Our characters don't have to be likeable. They have to be liveable. They have to have something about them that can be redeemed, whether that choice is taken. They don't have to be nice or pleasant or amenable or even-tempered. They can be bad and annoying and caustic and hateful. Keep us reading. Keep them alive. Keep them liveable.

If you can strike the balance for your characters so that they don't feel like characters in a book, and they feel real and lived, and they feel complex and nuanced and a mixture of light and shade and they have a story that will keep the readers going page after page, and we will love them, laugh with them hate them be frustrated by and ultimately fixated with them, and they feel real and liveable and like a loved one, if you can do that, and put words in their mouths that make them sound like people who speak words, yes I phrased that awkwardly to make a point about the importance of dialogue and cadence and all the rest of it, but yes, if you can do all that, my god, you've got a character for the ages.

Think of Spider-Man (oh boy, here we go with another Spidey reference). Sure, Peter Parker is nervous and guilty and shy and beleaguered and always getting things wrong. And with the mask on, he can be a hero, crack jokes, be cocky, be brave, be all the things he cannot be when he's plain old Puny Parker.

This is light and shade. If Parker was always miserable, if he didn't have an outlet for his funny side, his humane side, his heroic side, then he wouldn't be as enduring a character as he is.

Also, one-note characters are boring. They are. When I think back to villains from old comics, their wants and desires were always basic: steal the thing, get revenge on the superhero for stopping me steal the thing.

The genius of Thanos in the two *Avengers* films is that the first one (*Infinity War*) is about him and the second (*Endgame*) is about the heroes. We spend a lot of time trying to understand his reasons for doing what he does. We may not agree with them, but we understand them. To the point where Thanos talking about overcrowding in the universe and resources being wittered away by our greed and vanity, and how we should reset? That's something environmental activists talk about (without the genocide-y bit).

Thanos has a real-world concern. He kinda goes about it in the wrong way. He could be like Greta Thunberg and come up with a compelling reason to join a movement to do better. But no. He wakes up and chooses violence.

That is a complicated character. So complicated that we even get to see what he loses in order to achieve his goal.

He kills his daughter to get one of the infinity stones.

Suddenly, this is about life and death for him as much as it is for everyone else. He loses one of the only people he cares about to do what he thinks is right. Not only that, he chooses to lose that person. Once his daughter is dead, he has nothing left to lose. That's what makes him such a complex villain. And a brilliant villain. We have seen his torment. Now we understand why this is so important for him.

It's a good lesson for complicating our own cast of characters. Think about why they do what they do. See the world through their eyes. How do they justify the things they do? What do they want and what do they stand to lose, nay, what are they willing to lose, in order to achieve it?

Writing Prompt
(1 hour)

Write a diary entry for one of the other characters in your story, preferably someone who has done something bad to your protagonist. Try to justify it, try to see the world through their eyes, try to find their voice.

Interlude: Do you even need any of this advice?

Before we go on to the next part, I wanted to check in on how you're doing. Because we moved from Part 1 and getting those ideas down to some technical stuff about character. Now's a good time to see if u ok hun.

Wow. I've never sounded more like a dad of two there.

Remember how I wanted to reaffirm that writing is hard and you know the story you wish to tell better than anyone, but you must also know why you want to tell it, why you're the best person to tell it and why you need to tell it now?

Now is a good time for the latter because the former is probably troubling you right now. Let's think about instinct for a bit.

I cannot stress this enough: writing advice is great, but you are communicating with the cosmos.

Go with me on this briefly.

You know your story. You know it better than anyone. I cannot make it the best it can be. Only you can. Only your hard work and dedication and your thought and care, and your persistence and your communing with the cosmos.

Making stuff is all about extraction and communication. It's about presenting big ideas and conversations and aspects of the human condition to people. There is something in our communicating that cannot be taught. I can't teach you how to use words to bend our minds. I can't teach you how to write a sentence that turns a story on its head. An ending that makes us weep. An anecdote that makes us laugh.

All I'm doing is making the pool of technical knowledge as accessible as possible. There are creative writing teachers who will get you to think deeper than I have here. But this, what I present, is everything I think one should consider when it comes to story. But the actual function of writing means, to an extent, absorbing all this information, reflecting on it, tossing it to one side, and digging deep in order to commune with the cosmos.

I keep saying communing with the cosmos as a way of suggesting that the unknown, the thing at your core, that part of your soul you want to leave on the page for us to read for the rest of literature's lifespan, is something that only you can bring to the table.

There is something within us that compels us to tell stories. They help us understand the world, our selves, our nature, our place in . . . well, the cosmos. And it's easy to dismiss this. Think of it as unimportant. Consider it cliché. But it's true. What's the point otherwise? You're not reading this book because you're interested in intellectual pyrotechnics or linguistic gymnastics. You want to tell a story that sits within you as a better way of interrogating what's around you. That, my friend, is the cosmos of which I speak.

Whispers the cosmos is within you.

The point is, you know what you need to do. Trust your instinct. It's your best weapon as a writer. Without your instinct, you will find these writing tips, all writing advice, overwhelming. It's good to arm yourself with all this information. But I wrote three well-received novels before I even considered reading up on the science and craft of writing. Much of the storytelling was instinctual. And actually, when I was reading up on teaching craft, so I could, myself, teach, I realized that I had imbibed a lot of this from reading widely and spending a lot of time writing.

In 2009, I did a project that the comedian Josie Long was running, called '100 Days to Make Myself a Better Person'. The point was to do something for 100 days, preferably creative, to get you to look inwards and understand who you were and what you wanted to say. I did 100 days of writing stories about South Asians. There was a dearth of writing about British South Asians and their contemporary lives. Sometimes I used it as a journal, other times I followed a thought to see where it took me, others it was a character study, others it was a recollection of an anecdote, occasionally it got weird. There was a 500-word flash fiction piece called 'The Fudge Club', that was about snacking and elitism.

This is where I learned about how I tell stories, how to deploy humour, how to build up characters people care about. This was my training ground. I learned to write by writing a shitload. Sorry for the swear. But sometimes, you need one. For emphasis. Through writing and writing and reading and reading, I learned about the stories I was interested in telling and how I was going to tell them. I learned that genre wasn't the best use of my voice. That I love the space to be funny and to be sad. I love characters who are broken. I love watching people grow and come of age. I love stories set now. Right now. As we speak. I love writing about the city as a character. I love all of it.

But I wouldn't have discovered any of that without doing the work. Only you can tell the story that you want to tell in the way that you want to tell it. Only you have your unique perspective on the world and only you can create your cast of characters to populate it.

Trust your instinct.

Writing books like this is a comfort because sometimes they unlock bits of our instinct wrapped up in the cosmos. Sometimes they show us another way of digging deeper into our cosmos. Other times they make us realize we knew it already, all along.

I can't teach you how to write a joke. A joke can bypass your brain. A laugh is instinctual. A comedian couldn't sit with you and teach you how to make someone laugh. They could help you structure a stand-up set around your voice and give you an insight into how to pace and time jokes, and even suggest alternative punchlines. But you have to tell them. You have to deliver them and make us laugh and keep us entertained and enthralled. Only you can do that.

A songwriter can't necessarily teach you to write a hit song. A song can touch your soul, move you to dance, cry, smile, sing loudly, engage with that primal feeling within you that it elicits. A guitarist can teach you some chords. They can teach you how to play the rhythm guitar from 'Wonderwall', the riff from 'Voodoo Chile', the solo from an obscure Velvet Underground track. They could give you the basics of song structure. Teach you about melody and what notes to hit. But you have to write the song. And it's not a paint-by-numbers thing. Sure, the architecture of a song can give you parameters to operate within, but the reality is, it has to be performed with feeling.

Art is vocational. Something that improves the more you do it. Brain and heart, mind and soul – all that stuff – combines in a unique unquantifiable way. So, in short, reading this book, and all the other creative writing books, is great. Doing a course or a degree is super, but nothing beats showing up and putting one word down after the other.

Writing Prompt

Your prompt today is to put your story away and look at the next multiple-choice table, choose one from each column and do it:

A: DO SOMETHING
1.   Go for a walk in nature and get lost and find yourself.
2.   Go for a walk in the city and turn on to a street you've never been down.
3.   Go to a gallery or museum you like and stand in front of a painting (or go on their website and find a tour video).
4.   Go for a coffee with an old friend and ask them how they are and listen to their answers.
5.   Text an old friend a shared memory.

B: ENGAGE WITH SOME ART
1.   Read an essay from one of the open tabs you have on your browser/an essay you clicked on but never got time to read.
2.   Re-read the first twenty pages of one of your favourite books.
3.   Listen to a podcast documentary about something you need to research for your story.
4.   Watch an episode of a TV programme you've never seen before but everyone rates.
5.   Look through an old photo album. Either a physical one or pick a year from your archive/library and scroll through.

C: FIRST LINE OF YOUR 30-MINUTE PROMPT

1. 'She never knew it was going to be like this . . .'
2. 'It was at that moment, I knew I had to start a band . . .'
3. 'The first thing I do every day is . . .'
4. 'He stands against a wall, waiting, every day . . .'
5. 'I remember the time my mother told me . . .'

Go. Have fun. Today is about taking time away from the story. See you in the next part as we delve into some more technical stuff.

PART 4:
SETTING

N ow we've got the characters in our story established, we need to think about putting them into the world. That's what this short section is about.

Setting is the time and space your story exists in, the people who inhabit that world and the attitudes of the time. It can mean many things, but at its heart, it's time and space.

Before we start going into the specifics, let's take some time to go back to basics on setting. Answer these questions:

Where is your story set? (Break this down into universe, then galaxy, then planet, then continent, then country, then locale, then street if you need to . . .)

But where specifically is it set? Tell me about the street, the house, the town, the community. Think about the precincts available to you in the setting. The home? The school? The temple of eternity? Describe them. Visualize them. Make decisions about them. It's important you don't leave anything to chance. Forcing yourself to make decisions ensures that you're feeding character and plot and story. If they live in a home that's a certain way, surrounded by a community that's a certain way because of a time in history that was a certain way, that can ensure that you're making character and precinct be in conversation with each other.

Hold up, Shuks . . . what is a precinct?

Think of it as a specific space where action occurs. So in a house, we may have many rooms, but nothing happens in the corridor, the downstairs bog (if your characters are lucky to have a downstairs bog), the garden or the study. All the action is in the bedroom (ooooh baby) and the kitchen (oooooooh baby). These are your precincts. The dictionary (lol, imagine pulling the old dictionary definition trick on you) has precinct as 'the area within the walls or perceived boundaries of a particular building or place'. Don't think of the precinct as 13, Briar Close. Think of it as the specific rooms within 13, Briar Close.

Okay, next question: when is this set? The time period, the time of day, time of year. Was it early August in one particularly hot summer (2018) on Gloucester Road in Bristol? Was it Christmas in 1949? What was happening then? What can help you? What outside events have affected your characters and their community? How have they reacted to those outside events?

So now you know these things, so what? What does that add? Quite a lot. One of the first questions we need to ask ourselves with any novel is: why now? Not for us as the author, but for our protagonists. Why is this happening to them now? The setting can do a lot of the work in that regard. What the setting can give you in terms of the why now question is: a mood, an atmosphere, an external threat, something to protect, a home that is not what it seems. It can even be a character.

So how do we build on our setting?

It's easy (it's not, we have a whole part to get through, but you know, conceptually, it's easy). Be specific. Make a decision about the particular setting of each precinct your characters will come to occupy and fill that decision with specific details. Think of the history of a place and its people. Think of the buildings and what they look like and why they look like that. If you're writing about a place that's real, in a time that's real, do some research. Find out local history. Search online for photos from the time period you're writing. Is there a history book about the time or place you can read? Are there tour guides or videos? Can you visit it? Is that affordable? Does the setting affect how people spoke to each other? Do you know anyone from that area you can speak to?

Give the setting a purpose. If it's a house to escape to or a hometown to escape from or a citadel to reach or a beach where you once saw, fleetingly, the love of your life you thought to be dead . . . make the setting something that gives you purpose.

Writing Prompt
(30 minutes)

You have been commissioned to write one of those holiday pieces about a precinct in your novel. Choose either a home, a landmark or a site. Describe it in all its glory and foibles to your audience. You can choose what publication you're writing for. The aim of this is to understand the experience of visiting this place as an outsider. Because that is what your reader will be at first. You will learn how to bring them into the place.

Right, done? Let's dig into some setting things you need to consider.

Where do you go, my lovely?

As I mentioned, place can be the town, or the street, or the kitchen, or the country. Or all these things. You want the precincts in which your stories live to feel distinct and customized to the characters and their conflict. You want the spaces they occupy to feel lived-in and familiar to them, and even some readers. You want the place to be a character.

Now, unhelpful creative writing advice here: the place is a character. It sounds lovely, but what does it mean in practice? How do we do this?

Again, as I said earlier, it's about specificity. Specificity has to go beyond the Wikipedia page for the city your characters live in.

Imagine this was the opening to your book:

> Paul and Paula walked down the quaint Bristol street, not in love as they used to be. Bristol is a city and ceremonial county in England, United Kingdom. With a population of 463,400, it is the most populous city in South West England.

Boring, right?

Now try this:

Paul and Paula walked down the quaint Bristol street, not in love
as they used to be. Bristol is, as they say, for lovers. But what if
you've gone from lovers to flatmates? What then?

I've drawn out some detail about the feel of Bristol, one where
there are city-wide delusions of romance and adventure. And I've
mirrored the state of our main characters with this delusion, to set
us up for a story. When we meet them, they're not in love as they
used to be. And if Bristol is a city of love, how can we use the city
to recapture what they once had?

Place is about choice. It's a choice to set a story in a major city
because even then, cities comprise smaller villages with their own
community hovering around a centre they rarely venture to
because of *spits on ground* tourists. It's a choice to set a story in
a smaller town or village. To set it in a different country. Also, we
haven't even considered the time element of it. We'll get to that
shortly. What I want you to do is consider where this story is set.
And why. And what that gives you?

I can't offer you much expertise in genre world-building. It's
important to note what I am good at and not. So if you're writing
sci-fi or fantasy, I suggest you check out tips from people like
N. K. Jemisin, Tasha Suri and James Smythe.

My point still stands. Make the place mean something to the
characters and their journey. The easiest thing to do is reach for
where we grew up, or where we live now. There is that stereotype
of literary fiction being largely about unhappy marriages and
middle-aged, middle-class men feeling sad in North London,
because it's an easy reach for writers who aren't in the world
enough. Maybe they are and I'm making assumptions. The reality
is, I've got two young kids. How much am I in the world?

Here are some thoughts on how to write about a place, phrased
as questions to ask yourself.

How does this place make the characters feel? Are they at home here or strangers? Does that feeling change the longer they stay?

How does the architecture and geography of the place speak to something within them?

How was it decided that they would live here? In an essay by Hanif Abdurraqib I recently read the line: 'A country is something that happens to you. History is a series of thefts, or migrations or escapes, and along the way new bodies are added to a lineage.' Did this place happen to them? What does the history of this happening to them, be it coincident or purposeful, add to their sense of self?

What colour is the place?

What is the community like?

What is the architecture like and does it mirror the protagonists in our stories' journeys in any way?

What are the spaces that belong to everyone? What uses do they have? (This can apply to place being London, a suburb of London, a street in a suburb of London, a house on a street in a suburban of London, a room in a house on a street in a suburb of London; the more granular we can identify the precincts of your story, the more we are able to deploy them as a character.)

Here are some things you can do when thinking about place:

Look at old family photographs and home videos, if you have access to them, if they're relevant. These can be a real treasure trove of specificity. When were these photos taken? Note what everyone is wearing, doing, emoting, what is around them.

Head to the internet. I found a video of north-west London from the 1920s on an internet site recently. It wasn't what I was looking for. I was hoping for something earlier. I was so surprised to find it and to realize that the internet is definitely your friend.

Has anyone else written about the place you're describing? Are there poems, paintings, bursts of prose that capture the essence of the place? What do these all add to your sense of it? What can you note in addition? What can you add to your own perceptions of it?

Who can you talk to? If you're able to. Are there oral histories you can find, people you can interview or have informal chats with? I found, last year, in trying to piece together fragments of the house I lived in in that time of childhood amnesia, before I was four, I relied on my father and kaki sending me voice notes on a popular messaging app, about the architecture and furniture of the house. I could remember where the door was and the stairs and the rooms downstairs, but I couldn't quite picture the kitchen or upstairs. I have a vague memory of watching my kaki unpack a suitcase when she moved in with us, having just married my kaka. They could remember different bits of the house, and that gave me a new perspective on it. Now, that house didn't end up featuring in the text, but the sense of home did, and also Google Street View gave me something unrecognizable.

Can you go and visit it? That seems like the easiest way to do it.

An aside here: writing place in historical fiction requires a level of research that one should not take lightly. In order to create a sense of place, you have to be able to write about it in the time that it was set. We'll speak a bit more about time in the next section, but I wanted to draw your attention to the fact that photographs, oral accounts and paintings are definitely the best pieces of evidence for you. Also, if you have a small budget, you can find an expert in the time period to help you. It's important to compensate people who help you with research, especially if they are doing it as a job. Historians, experts in certain professions, obsessives of certain artefacts and lifestyles, they are all sharing their expertise with you, and sometimes there is a limit to what you can research by yourself, and certainly a limit to what you can find online, and not everyone has access to a local library, let alone something like the British Library, and not everyone can afford heaps of academic textbooks and art books and photography books, so maybe it's worth finding someone and paying for their time. And if the cost of paying for their time is a factor, research funding applications for writers, which do exist, that help you with researching and writing your book.

Authenticity matters. As I said earlier, the thing is: your readers have to trust you to take them on a journey. The moment they lose trust in you, you lose them as a reader. A way for you to lose their trust is by badly researching something, making assumptions instead of deploying facts, not understanding things like procedure and process in certain professions. And so on and so forth.

In summation, writing about place is all about specificity and utilizing it the right amount. Paragraphs of glorious, languid description are great. But how much does it keep a reader engaged?

Writing Prompt
(30 minutes)

Write about the place you grew up in. The rule is you are not allowed to give me any physical description of any rooms or things in the house (as in, don't use any adjectives to describe anything). Tell me the feeling of each room. Give me a tour through the emotional resonances of each room of the place you grew up in.

Who will write about this place if I don't?

I was asked to write about the London suburb I grew up in for a newspaper column once. And I wrote about how its stifling energy and conventional structure made it a place for creativity, a place to create excitement. How its streets fed my books. Because walking these streets were ordinary people doing extraordinary things, everypeople excavating small moments of grace in their lives. It felt so strange writing about the place I was so desperate to leave when I was growing up, and the place I was excited to return to four or five times a year to see family, though I rarely if at all left my relatives' houses to experience being in my old manor. I couldn't see how it changed or how it was still the same.

I was at a dinner, six months after writing about Harrow, and a musician I absolutely adored, who grew up near me, was there. I was scared to talk to him because I thought he was cool and mysterious. But as he hovered over the hummus, waiting for me to finish spooning some onto my plate, he leaned in and said, 'You're that bredrin who wrote about Harrow in the *Guardian*, innit?'

I smiled and said, yes, that was me. I couldn't believe he had read it.

He said, 'Part of me was like, why would anyone want to write about growing up in Harrow in the *Guardian* of all places . . .' He paused. Then added, 'but then if you don't write about that place, who will?'

Often I see my role as writer to be part-archivist. The only thing people know about Harrow is that there's a posh school on a hill there and they all wear weird boating hats and that's it. Harrow for me is so ordinary. It's a suburb filled with immigrants and the insular community they've created, gentrification as the luxury apartment industrial complex heads into the outer zones of the Tube lines, an old guard of anti-fascists, a lot of civil servants, and the posh people in weird boating hats at the top of the hill.

It doesn't quite mesh together and yet it perfectly encapsulates the incongruousness of city living. And this guy was right. If I didn't write about this place, who would? And what would they say?

The way Zadie Smith writes about place, whether it be in *NW* or any of her other books, she has mined the ordinariness of the suburbs she writes about to create something magical. Of course she is writing about the tensions of race and class and casual violence and untapped potential. And the London she writes about is conscious and alive, filled with the sights, smells and sounds I asked you to home in on. The line 'Sweet stink of the hookah, couscous, kebab, exhaust fumes of a bus deadlock' brings everything back to me. I am home in that moment. I am in London, though I left ten years ago. I am in the city I live in now and I am seeing, smelling, hearing the same things. It's the consistency of sense that keeps these places alive and instils in us a desire to archive those places that made us.

Because if we don't write about these places, who will?

Writing Prompt
(2 hours)

Write an essay about the town/village/city/street you grew up in. Pick a particular moment at a particular time in a particular year and tell me everything about that moment in that place and how it changed you and how it changed how you view the place. It may be about leaving, it may be about coming home, it may be about falling down and a community coming together around you. It may be a bad event. It may be a positive event. But it must be a moment of change in a place that felt different immediately after that change.

If you can't think of anything to do with the place you grew up in, think about the place you are in now (if that's different).

How good am I at geography?

Unless you're good at geography, we don't need to know everything you know about geography. That's not how we consider setting.

It's not interesting to tell me what the population of your place is, or what its longitudinal and latitudinal coordinates are. I don't need to know it's the fifth-largest whatever in wherever. What I want to know is, how does it feel to leave here, for your characters? I don't need the rainfall statistics or the climate conditions. Not unless it tells me something about the characters. There is textural padding to hit daily word counts, and there is characterful detail that makes me understand choice and circumstance. A particularly rainy city experiencing a drought and a hot summer might result in tensions. A place being rural might mean that people are more willing to try it and get away with it. A small town might give our character the fateful small-town syndrome. A big city might be the perfect place for our characters to arrive as strangers, or to have grown up and now seen how it is changing, or leave briefly only to return and view it with fresh eyes.

We might want to know the type of neighbourhoods they exist in and the types of people they're going to walk past, the types of environments they are part of, and what people within those environments want or need. And this should always be related to plot and to story.

It's not an excuse to cut and paste from the internet. It's not an excuse to do a geography lesson. I have the utmost respect for geography teachers. They have a hard job trying to make kids care about the world in a way that doesn't seem abstract to them, and people make fun of them. But you're writing literature, story, a feat of wonder and brilliance. Not giving us a lesson on cumulus clouds.

Unless the cumulus cloud is actually an alien headed for earth.

Writing Prompt
(30 minutes)

Write a short piece of fiction about a cumulus cloud coming to invade Earth.

Creeeeeak: is somebody there?

I am going to tread lightly in this bit. I don't read or watch horror. Here's a confession for you. When I was little, maybe nine, I watched *Carry On Screaming* with my friends and it freaked me the hell out. Yeah, go on, laugh like you've never been irrationally scared by something that's actually silly; no, that shadow on your bedroom ceiling never made you run into another room.

I wasn't emotionally ready for the scary bits of *Carry On Screaming*. Nor was I for the funny bits. I've not seen it since, so I couldn't tell you if it was funny.

There's a bit where one of the werewolves gets their finger severed. I can't even remember the circumstances. I could look up the plot synopsis online, but why put myself through such trauma to make a point about haunted houses? The finger is found by the bad guys – I think Kenneth Williams is one of them – and they put the finger in a machine. It generates a second werewolf. I don't know what it was about this idea, but it terrified me. I couldn't look at the screen. I haven't watched horror since.

Except for a recent film called *His House*. Directed by Remi Weekes, *His House* is about a refugee couple who make a harrowing escape from war-torn South Sudan, but then they struggle to adjust to their new life in an English town that has an

evil lurking beneath the surface. It's terrifying. A mixture of
social commentary (which most obsessive horror fans will tell
you is often the point of the genre) and shocks and terror, it's
a brilliant film that I braved at 11 am on a Tuesday. I tried to
think of the most harmless part of the week. And it was definitely
broad daylight, late morning on an inconsequential day of
the week.

What struck me most about the film, other than the terror it
puts you through, and let's say I won't be rushing back to the
genre any time soon, was its use of space as a character. The
house of the title was such a menacing force. It had a life of
its own.

It was outstanding in its usage of place. I know this is a trope in
the genre, the idea of the haunted house as a character.

I wanted to take you through my learning so you can think about
bringing your own enclosed spaces alive.

1. There can't be too many exits. In fact, only one way in and
    one way out.
2. The seemingly cute or quaint or innocent objects (e.g. a
    shelf of dolls) must look malevolent in the wrong light.
3. There is always one room that's different from the rest.
4. You can get a lot of mileage out of a locked door that
    seemingly has no reason to be locked.
5. What is crawling between the walls?
6. What everyday sounds can terrify in the wrong context?
7. You are always being watched in a house that's alive.
8. There is the sense that you are not the only ones in a
    house that's alive.
9. A house's history is set in stone. But a house can be
    adaptable to new circumstances.

10. What tragic things have happened in this house? What trauma stains its floorboards?

Writing Prompt
(1 hour)

Bring your character home after a long day. Something is amiss in their home. What is it and what does this mean for them? Play into the horror context, scare them a bit, make them anxious that this home is not what they thought.

Is this a dead-end town in a dead-end world?

I'm offering up a few extreme settings for you to think about as they may relate to your own experiences and those of your protagonists.

So your setting might be a familiar place, or it might be a new place. This isn't necessarily coincidental or relying on tropes. Imagine this: there is an infinite number of stories to be told about a city; the protagonist of your story is one, and it is unique to them and their worldview.

Here, we're going to think about how a familiar place, and the desire to leave, can be a catalyst for a journey.

Often, the moment of change comes to our characters at a point where they feel like they've outgrown the place they live in. The spaces where we grow up we have such a love/hate relationship with. I hated where I grew up and now I look back on it nostalgically. My sister, on the other hand, never left, never entertained it as an option.

Sometimes characters need to leave a place to come back again, changed, so they can look out anew across familiar fields with fresh eyes. Think of Frodo's return to the Shire and how different he feels, though everything he left has remained the same. Think of when Connell returns to Sligo and falls into old patterns. And so on.

I want us to consider how a town or a city or a village might reflect the rot at our protagonist's heart, giving them pause to consider leaving.

However, the sad truth of these places is that they don't make it easy for you to leave. So let's build up the mythology of the place.

1. Is your protagonist happy to be there? Are the other residents? What are the traditions and routines that fester in this space? How do they point to a way things are done?
2. How do they treat outsiders?
3. Who are the local heroes and what are they known for?
4. Who has left and never come back? How are they viewed?
5. What is this place known for outside of this place? What would an outsider know about it?
6. What would most people's ambitions be here? How does this differ from your protagonist?
7. Who does your protagonist get on with here? Why? Where do they feel safe and welcome?

This isn't about writing a crappy town. This is about understanding how place is about the people who make it a place and how their attitudes can fix the position of our protagonist. This could work from aristocracy to village, from castle to space station, from made-up island to seaside town, where the only opportunities are to work in the family business. This is about establishing how the people influence the way the place is and how that pushes our protagonist to try to leave. Or be happy to stay.

No writing prompt to end this bit. Just sit with those questions. Maybe, if you can, take a walk around the area you're trying to recreate in words.

What's the time?

Hilary Mantel said something amazing about writing historical
fiction in her Reith Lecture. And it's applicable to so much of the
way we view writing.

> Evidence is always partial. Facts are not truth, though they are
> part of it – information is not knowledge. And history is not the
> past – it is the method we have evolved of organizing our
> ignorance of the past. It's the record of what's left on the record.
> It's the plan of the positions taken, when we stop the dance to note
> them down. It's what's left in the sieve when the centuries have
> run through it – a few stones, scraps of writing, scraps of cloth. It
> is no more 'the past' than a birth certificate is a birth, or a script is
> a performance, or a map is a journey. It is the multiplication of the
> evidence of fallible and biased witnesses, combined with
> incomplete accounts of actions not fully understood by the people
> who performed them. It's no more than the best we can do, and
> often it falls short of that.

Let's use this to think about the time you're setting this. Let's
consider this. When is this set and who are our characters when

this is set? Considering what Mantel refers to as the sieve, how can we root our characters in a specific time and place?

Setting something in the present day can be nebulous if the now isn't a fixed point. Phones change, methods of communication change, clothes styles change, the way we speak changes. I was conscious, when my second novel came out, that even though it was about identity curation online, an issue for the ages, as it got older, it would date for some readers because of the platform I chose to base the whole thing around. But for me, it rooted it in that time. I don't find myself pulled out of a Jane Austen novel every time a letter is written. I'm not reading it for the letter writing. I'm reading it for the characters and how they communicate with each other. It's like, if your readers are poking under the hood, maybe that's because the chasse isn't compelling enough. If you give your readers a reason to pull themselves out of the text, then you've ultimately failed as an author. It shouldn't matter to them whether your characters are writing letters, using AIM, tweeting, TikToking or using a weird made-up site called ChatPal. Your job is to immerse them in the moment.

So, picking a fixed time can date a book. But that dating can prove essential. I know where I am if the book is set in the summer after the Brexit referendum, or if it's set in 2012 and we're all excited about the Olympics, or in the late eighties and everyone's driving around in Ford Cortinas moaning about Thatcher. It lends an authenticity to the time. And much as authenticity isn't something that should paralyze an author when it comes to their sense of self, authenticity of world as it relates to character is important.

Time isn't about giving historical information to your reader. It's about the way your characters view the world. They may not know they're in a significant war because it's happening around them, and actually, all they care about is whether her father is going to recover from his medical condition. They won't necessarily know all the political movements of the time because of access to information or desire to know. I know the running joke, 2016 to now, is about how we are constantly noting that we live in historical and unprecedented times, and this is partly to do with how the internet, and, in particular, social media, has primed us to narrate the complexities of our lives in real time rather than sitting and reflecting on them, but most characters in things don't know that, outside, history is happening. And if they do, how does it relate to their world? Work all this out before you start cutting and pasting details from Wikipedia.

In their world, what does the time mean to them? What impact would socio-political events, global events, national or local events have on their lives, on where they live and what specifically about them would this say?

Also, now you're thinking about place, time to start thinking about how the time affected the place.

What does life look like?

We talked earlier about establishing the flow of things for a character before preparing to disrupt it with our point of attack. We know what their life looks like and we know how we're going to throw them off course.

But how do we ensure that our characters' lives do feel disrupted in some way? What can we do to make their lives feel real?

Think about time not as a moment in time, but also in terms of how time places our protagonist in the flow of things.

Think about how your characters pass the time before the story starts and how they fill their days. How well do they sleep? What are their patterns? What are their regular mealtimes? Are they long and languorous, or are they on the hoof? What is their work situation? How do they pass the days? Get to work and be forced to leave? Clock-watcher? How do they alleviate boredom? What is their down time? What is their leisure time? What is their attitude to time? A glass-half-empty kinda archetype might be the sort of person to spend a lot of time doing passive things, whereas a regular go-getter has a goal in their sights, and they won't rest until they achieve it. When they lie down to rest, what do they file from their day? The passage of mundanity can give us things to contend with. The opportunity for conflict.

Imagine, the divorced dad who every Tuesday picks his kid up from school and takes them out for food, but he has landed a huge client, or he's asked out the girl of his dreams, or an alien has told him he is the one and he must accompany them on the quest. Suddenly we have to think about his poor kid, standing outside school like a lemon, a worried lemon who doesn't know how they're getting home. Tick tick tick.

Imagine the person who goes to work every day, zombie eyes, slow trudge, uniform of depression, fed up with the drudgery of life. What is different about today? How is today's routine ever so slightly different and how will it throw them off course?

Imagine that moment where you decided to break up with that person and this essay is about what happened after your break-up, your journey to healing. Establish the routines of the relationship. Show us how it will disrupt your life.

Imagine that story you're writing about a real person who did something miraculous or awe-inspiring or worthy of documenting in prose. Establish what their life looked like, the passage of time that led them to this moment. Was it inevitable, given their path so far, or was it inevitable in reaction to their surroundings?

Imagine documenting the day; remember the routine. Establish the routine. Don't skip over the routine. When you review your journals later on down the line, you will be able to see who you were and reflect on where you are now only through establishing your routine.

Routine is about the patterns of life, how they may be disrupted, and what that may add to the urgency of the plot. Routine is about time spent in a life lived. How well do you know your characters if you don't know their routine? How they get up, what their attitude to meals is, whether they move to the tick and the tock of a clock, or whether they are chaotic. Time spent gives us the insight we need into how our characters work and how our world operates. Here, we may find insights into their socio-political position. Whether they drive to work or have no work. Whether they fill their own time or have every second of the day already accounted for, and spent by others. What their homes look like and what happens in the morning, at night. What moves through and they don't blink an eye. What might be useful to know later. What might seem out of the ordinary.

We have to leave nothing to chance.

Establish their routine.

Here's how:

When do they wake up and how?

What is the first thing they think? Are they springing out of bed or emerging slowly?

What is urgent about their morning? What isn't?

Do they have somewhere to be? How do they prepare to set themselves up for the day/night? What do they eat? What do they put on? What are their rituals?

How do they get to where they need to be? Who else might they encounter? Who or what might greet them on arrival?

Are they welcome here? Do they welcome being here?

What is their attitude to the things that need to be done?

We could keep moving through their day. All the way through to bedtime. What do you think this might give you? Because, if you're disrupting this world, you are potentially disrupting this routine. It might give your protagonist something to want to return to, something that has made them the way they are, or more importantly, everyone else carried on as normal.

The wider world, with the passage of time in space, might not know that our hero is engaged in a dangerous love affair or a fight to the death.

All they know is 'I gotta get these expense reports in by the end of the day or I'll get a formal disciplinary'.

Writing Prompt
(1 hour)

Pick someone who is not the main person in your story, not the protagonist and not the narrator. Give us a blow-by-blow, specific account of their day. Show us what their world looks like. Try to understand and expand the world of your story through the perspective of someone else.

Do my characters tweet?

Let's move on to a modern-day story problem: Twitter. Instagram. TikTok. Whatever platform is big at the point you read this.

Do they need a place in our stories?

If you're writing something contemporary, ignore social media at your peril. People use these sites. They get their news, their social interactions, their opinions, their laughs and their anxieties from them. Sometimes relying too much on the ebb and flow of notifications can impact on a character's journey if they're not in the world enough. So it's important, as a writer, to strike a balance between the realistic existence of social media in a character's world as well as real-world interactions.

I've read books that heavily incorporate social media usage into the text, using it as a way of discussing identity, fractured realities, our sense of self. Others weave social media into the text seamlessly. Specifically, look at how the main character of *Luster* by Raven Leilani scrolls aimlessly as a way of exhibiting her boredom, the rut she's in. Whereas in *Leave the World Behind*, by Rumaan Alam, in which a family staying in a rural location endures a signal outage. The lack of ability to scroll, to look up answers to questions, get the news, adds to the sense of paranoia. So while Alam is writing about the absence of social media, he is using it to demonstrate how we live now and how we would react in a catastrophe where we can't access up-to-the-second information about it.

So let's do this as a set of questions to ask yourself:

1. What are your characters' relationships with social media? Be specific. What sites do they use and what for? How does their usage make them feel? How much of their day is consumed by usage? What sort of following do they have? What sort of interactions do they get? Are they on there for validation or information, for snooping or for shitposting, for news gathering or news disseminating?
2. What would a significant post for them look like? What would an everyday one look like?
3. How do others around them view their usage?
4. If you took their phone away, how would they react?
5. What about their private messages? Who are they in text conversations with? About what? What is the level of intimacy between them and the person? What group chats are they in?

Now, how do you wish to record this on the page? Is it a case of reportage?

For example:

Paul lay on his bed, scrolling mindlessly, reading Twitter threads on Mandalorian spoilers. The text from Mike lay unanswered in his WhatsApp, a pulsating grenade he tried to distract himself away from. He liked a few memes about Baby Yoda and replied to a few people asking when his flower shop would reopen. He then went back to WhatsApp and stared at Mike's text. He dropped his phone on his bed and rolled over to stare at the ceiling.

Or:

> Paul lay on his bed, scrolling mindlessly through Twitter.
>
> *Loving season 2 of #themandalorian but when's Baby Yoda gonna be a teen? [insert some emojis here]*
>
> *#themandalorian season finale is so sick. No spoilers but I [poop emoji] myself. IYKYK. LOL.*
>
> The text from Mike was still in his WhatsApp.
>
> *What are you up to?*
>
> A pulsating grenade. He tried to distract himself by liking a few Baby Yoda memes.

What feels real to your character and their world? The reported style? The more formal, 'putting the things in the thing' style? There are other ways to incorporate the world of social media into your prose. But the key is being honest about how it all relates to who is on it.

Writing Prompt
(30 minutes)

Write a twenty-tweet thread from the perspective of your character about something they care about.

Be anachronistic if you need to be. The more fun and frivolous the better!

#go.

The point of this exercise is to have fun and put the people in your story in a context other than the one you're used to!

Interlude: Is your blood on the page?

A lot of writers talk about the importance of voice, so I'm going to talk to you about the importance of soul. Because the best writing, the writing that moves, excites, commiserates, calms, saddens or breaks the heart of the reader, the writing that makes them laugh and cry and gasp and sigh and pump a subtle fist at their waist in celebration is the writing that bleeds on the page.

It's the only way I know how to write and the only thing I like to read. I'm not interested, as a writer, in intellectual gymnastics. I am not bothered by experimentation for its own sake. I cannot spend time with characters who are cyphers for an author's grandstanding political point. I want your blood on the page.

Sure, other writers, other readers, will disagree. But this is my book. All I can tell you is my truth.

Because otherwise, what is the point of this big undertaking? Why write a story? A novel is, as the old saying goes, a sculpture you've made after many attempts to shovel sand into a box. A novel is a moment in time, a mirror, a window, a powerful way of understanding the world and the people in it. But also, a novel is a piece of your soul, on the page, for everyone to hold within themselves. It is the way you see the world and the way you see yourself and the way you see us. It's your interrogation of the universe.

I first started writing my third novel, *The One Who Wrote Destiny*, in 1999. I was hung up on a story I'd heard about my family. My uncle had fought a landmark legal case in the late sixties, and had in the process done something to make lives better for non-white people in this country. He stood up against a piece of everyday racial discrimination and condemned it. It went to court and while the decision didn't go his way, the entity in question changed a company policy they held. As one man, he made a difference and made my life easier. What a hero. I wanted to write a book about him. All I had to go on were summarized snapshots of conversation about what had gone on. It wasn't a story because I was telling someone's story, not my own, and I was telling it as factually as I could. I wrote 10,000 turgid words and gave up because it was such a disservice to my uncle.

Years later, I realized that what I was lacking was characters, so I tried again. This time, I made the characters big, larger than life, complete with foibles and slapstick reactions. I made the action farcical, and I wrote with whimsy. Again, it wasn't working. I showed it to my then agent and her assistant gave it the death knell. Her reply was akin to a cut-and-paste rejection you'd have if it was an unsolicited manuscript, rather than a thoughtful response to a book by a client her boss represented. Humiliated, I parted ways with the agent and parked the book.

Years after that, I found myself on a lot of trains, to and from venues where I'd rock up, talk about *The Good Immigrant* and come home. Something happened on those train journeys home. Having spent an entire evening talking about racism, and feeling on edge because it's hard to talk about the trauma of such things night after night, I found myself always heading home to my children, on a late train, two hours or so to myself, and I would feel vulnerable and stressed and I would comfort eat and write my novel. The vulnerability and depression I was feeling at the time unlocked something in me. I knew what I needed to do to make the book good. Now it was called *A Man, Without a Donkey*.

I realized what these characters needed. They needed for me to bleed on the page. Often we think about giving our characters wants and desires, and stakes. What will it mean for them if they don't get what they want or need.

What about the author? What are my stakes? If I didn't write this book, what would it mean for me? Just to remind you of the three questions a friend of mine asks themselves before working on a thing: does this stretch me? Does this stretch culture? Is me doing this the difference between it happening and not?

Answering the last question shook me. If I didn't write this story about my uncle, and about the intergenerational conversation I wanted to have about immigration, then who would write it? And would they write it with my unique take and worldview?

If I didn't write it, it wouldn't exist. Those were the stakes for me. It became life or death, and I wrote the book on those trains, putting twenty years of expectation about what it could be into the book. And I ended up with my third novel. One where I said everything I needed to about immigration.

I always say about all my books: 'I gave it my all.' And it's true. It was true of my third novel and every one I've written. It's especially true of the memoir, because with *Brown Baby* I couldn't hide emotional truth behind fiction, behind made-up people occupying made-up spaces. I had to put the emotional truth front and centre and curate the events from my own life in order to show it. *Brown Baby* is my blood on the page. It means that whatever anyone says about it, I know that I put everything into it. It stretched me to write it, and it'll stretch culture by widening the conversation on some of the themes discussed. If I hadn't written it, then who would have done?

So, my challenge to you is to bleed on the page. Write each thing you work on like it's life or death. Because these works will exist forever, and if they contain small chips of our soul within them, then we will make our mark on the world. Don't write to play at intellectual gymnastics. Write like you are communicating with the world, all your joy and pain, and it was the only book you could have written in that instance.

Writing Prompts

We've been working on some technical stuff and I bet it's been hard. It is hard. It's definitely hard. I don't want you to lose the love of writing, so before we move from thinking about what our stories could be, to getting them out of our brains and onto the page, and on to the next section, which is looking at our stories and working out the best way to make them the best we can possibly make them, let's have some fun.

What follows is five situations, five first lines and five themes. Interpret them as you want. My advice would be, have fun, and write in your comfort zone, but also, pick one to do that is against what you usually write. So if you write sci-fi usually, try a personal essay, and vice versa. These are prompts without consequence. They exist to help you keep writing and loving writing.

FIVE SITUATIONS

1. Two people arrive at the same place. They aren't expecting to see the other person.
2. A time when you had to deal with a situation that compromised you in some way.
3. After years of doing the right thing, and getting nowhere, they decided to do the wrong thing for once.
4. An event in your life that hurt at the time but now feels like your origin story.
5. If they didn't go for it now, right now, they never would.

FIVE FIRST LINES

1. 'When it arrived, the package was damaged . . .'
2. 'I'll try not to embarrass you,' he said, packing his bag.
3. 'Every time he looked at it, he felt a tinge of regret . . .'
4. 'Across town, people were slowly disintegrating into dust . . .'
5. 'I didn't ever think my life would end up like this . . .'

FIVE THEMES

1. Good versus evil.
2. Love.
3. Redemption.
4. Coming of age.
5. Revenge.

Ten ways to take a break, writer style

How to take a break from writing in ways that still count as writing:

1. Go for a walk and think about your characters.
2. Re-read the thing that spurred you on to finally tell your story.
3. Write a postcard to a friend you haven't connected with in a while.
4. Write a list of ten things you know you're good at.
5. Have a shower. The best ideas come in the shower. Or the bath. Or a pool. Find a body of water, get in it, meditate as the water envelops you.
6. Cook a meal that reminds you of a specific time, place or person.
7. Find interviews with your favourite writers, be they online, in journals and magazines or podcasts. Listen to them. See what genius you can absorb.
8. Try another writing prompt.
9. Do none of these things. Lie on your bed. Close your eyes. Have a nap.
10. Drink water.

PART 5:

HOW DO I EDIT MY WORK?

Writing is rewriting, as people often say. Someone once told me that first drafts are like shovelling sand into a sandbox, from which you will eventually make sand sculptures. And there is a real truth to this. You are in control of when you show others your work. You've spent an amount of time putting your soul on the page; don't expect it to be ready to show others yet. Take your time. Time away from the manuscript. The characters. The world. Your own vulnerability.

Now we have worked up our story, and we've taken a break, let's spend some time back in the technical world. Let's think about how to take a first draft and make it a better second draft. We called it 'draft zero' earlier. Now we're going to work on draft one.

The first time you commit your story to paper, it's about realizing an idea. The next draft is about making sense of it for yourself. Then each draft after that, if this is the path you go down, helps you get it further from you, towards your readers.

The worst time to begin an edit is immediately after finishing a draft, when you're still basking in completion euphoria.

Don't do it. You rushed the end. You know the middle needs fixing. You know the beginning needs a rewrite because of where you ended up.

A first draft that takes six months to write needs six months at least to edit. Give yourself time. You're not in a rush. This story is going to exist forever. Why rush it? Often we have to ascertain the difference between 'this is finished' and 'I need to get it off my desk'.

These are conflicting emotions.

'This is finished' means: I can no longer do anything else to this to make it better. I am moving commas around. I can no longer see the wood for the trees. I am done.

Let's sit here for a second. 'I can no longer see the wood for the trees' doesn't mean this is finished. It means I am taking a break and I need someone external to the book to give me their thoughts. This is important. If you're able to find other writers who can read your work (and you theirs), you have a golden, brilliant opportunity. 'I can no longer see the wood for the trees' means I can get an outside perspective. Sharing work with other writers can be empowering because their feedback can either give you something you haven't felt before or it can crystallize what you want the book to be. Being finished can often feel like an unattainable goal. We'll go into how to know when something is finished shortly. Because it is different from 'I can no longer do anything else to make this matter'.

'I need to get this off my desk' is you not taking the time to take stock of any of the above. Frustration or elation means you're not taking too much care of your work. Once you finish a draft, give yourself a week or so off it before deciding to do anything with it. Honestly.

There are a bunch of different edits to do. I'm going to focus on a bunch of things in this section that you may not consider about editing. The first is that there are different types of editing that need to be done. I'll tell you how to approach each one, but the main thing to remember is, different edits are for different things.

The first thing to say is there is time to sweat the big stuff and time to sweat the small stuff. Time to consider the massive overarching things and time to move commas.

So what are the different edits?

Think of an edit like this: you start with the universe and you move smaller and smaller, to galaxy, then to planet, then to continent, then to country, then to city, then to area, then to street. It is a process of getting closer and closer to the line with each editorial pass. And you will need multiple passes to get your story right.

1. **The Structural Edit:** This is where you only think about the big-picture things like story, character, plot, setting, pace. Here you think about the protagonists of your story and whether we are seeing their journey in its fullest potential. Are the obstacles they face thematically linked to their story? Are they believable? Are they interesting? Do we want to follow them through the plot? Don't worry about the small things. Only the big ones. Do as many of these structural edits as you need because when you start moving things around, adding story in, changing elements of the plot, it can unravel the thread of your story. So remember to do multiple structural passes where you think of the big, big stuff.

2. **The Copyedit**: Once you're happy with your story, you need to think about the smaller stuff, like dialogue, like adverb-overuse, like long, languid descriptive passages, like whether there is that particular branch of bank on that street in that town, like whether elements of the world are consistent. You focus on the line-by-line of it all. You get close to the words and you read them aloud and you make

sure that one sentence flows into the next one. You make sure you aren't using unnecessary adjectives. You make sure each sentence justifies its weight in the story.

3. **The Proofread:** This is where you may have done multiple passes, three or four structural edits, one or two copyedits. Now the proofread, the final read. Don't let your eyes glaze over and skim because you've done this multiple times. Sure, you're moving commas, correcting the occasional spelling mistake, but at this point, it should feel like the story you wish to be out in the world.

My main advice with the three edits is: take them stage by stage, be prepared to do this multiple times, be prepared for things to still not feel right, be prepared to take your time away from the draft if you need a bit of space and objectiveness. You are your best critic but also, you – and by 'you' I mean 'I' – know that when a task is big and overwhelming, you can take shortcuts to get it off your desk. So allow yourself the time. I'm being harsh and particular here because it's taken you so long to get to this point. You wrote a story! And you've taken the decision that you want that story to exist and be read. You don't want to fart out an edit. You want to take as long as you did with the first draft in the edit, if not longer. Your story deserves this gift of time and close reading.

How do I approach an edit?

Editing is hard. Harder than writing the first draft, and that was really, really hard. Editing is hard because as soon as you finish your first draft, you're elated . . . you're on top of the world and you want to dive straight in again and edit it and send it to four million literary agents and . . . stop. Just stop for a second. Stop. Here's how to approach an edit.

Take. Your. Time. Friend. Just take your time. It took you [x] months to write the first draft. Why rush the edit? Again, the amount of time spent on your edit should correlate with how long it took you to finish the first draft. Just to adapt slightly what I said before about the various stages: the first draft is about filling the page with an idea. The second is about getting the story sorted, the characters living and breathing, and the plot in place. It's about sorting out the structural issues. The third draft might be about pace, dialogue, character journeys. The fourth might then be about moving commas around. Then you might feel like you can do nothing else to it. Then you can send it off. But, the time to begin the second draft isn't in the minutes after finishing the first one. The time to start the second draft is . . . sometime in the future.

Put. The. Draft. In. The. Proverbial. Drawer.

Take a month off, minimum. Do other writing. Think about the next book. Think about this one. But at a distance. Watch all seven seasons of *The Good Wife*. Trust me.

In this time off, the following things will happen:

1. You will itch to get back to it.
2. You will have realizations about plot, story, character.
3. You'll have five amazing ideas that seem award-winning one day, all nice and shiny, and then hard and not as good as the story you've already completed the next.
4. You will find a liminal space between you as a writer and you as a reader and this is going to help you edit. Because the thing people tend to forget when they work on their stories is that being a reader helps you be a better writer.
5. You will think, Oh god, if I don't get this done I will never do it.
6. You will then enter a stage of calm, knowing that it's there, and it's ready for you.
7. You will be irritated at the thought of going back to it. It's summer, time to light the barbecue.
8. You will get a notification on your calendar: it's time. You'll purse your lips, narrow your eyes, wrinkle your nose and get to it.
9. You will read those intentions you wrote at the time, reminding you why this, why you, why now. You will remember what is at the heart of the story.

    Now, you're ready.

Ready?

Okay, here's the next list of things to do. Editing is partly going to work and doing your job, partly being a creative genius and partly being a smart reader of yourself. In terms of going to work and doing your job, this is about putting in the hours. Yes, it's hard work, but showing up is all you need to do. Show up and do what needs to be done. Being a creative genius is being prepared to unravel things, do significant rewrites and not feel too overwhelmed by how much needs doing. Being a creative genius is knowing what's best for your story, knowing you know it best and being prepared to rip it up and start again if needs be. And being a smart reader? Well, here's a top tip: read your work before you begin your edit of it.

Here's the flow of it:

1. Print the manuscript off, booklet style. If you don't have a printer at home, time to sneak in early to work, or pay a fiver to a printing place, or arrive at a printer-friend's house with a cake and a big 'I love you, pal' smile.

    Printing your work out is important. (I know I'm assuming access to printers. Sorry! I don't even have a printer. I go to a shop.) The point of this is to make it look like a book. Because next you need to . . .

2. Read it. Take a week to experience your book as a reader. Read it through. In its entirety. Don't make any notes. Do not mark the page. DO NOT edit as you go. Just read it and experience it as a reader might for the first time. You are a reader first and a writer second. You arrived on the page having spent so long on others. And now you're ready to tell your own stories, you have to acknowledge that your greatest strength is arriving here because you love reading. You know what you like and don't like. You have read books people rave about and shrugged. You have pressed a book into someone else's hand and whispered, urgently, 'Read this.' You know what you like and don't. You know the difference between stories that move you and stories that

don't. So before you make any changes to your story, trust yourself as a reader. Read the book all the way through. On a practical level, it gives you the big picture of what needs to be done. If you go line by line, from chapter one, without rereading, you have no idea what needs fixing until it arrives and you might end up most of the way through before understanding what needed attention nearer the start.

3. Once finished, you may write down all the structural notes you need to in a letter to yourself. All the things that need to change. But only when you finish. This way, your notes are about the big picture. Fixing things all the way throughout. Your first significant edit isn't concerned with what's happening in the sentences. Only in the story. This ensures that you don't get to page 150 on your Word doc and think, crap, I have to go back to page 3. This allows you to think about the whole of the novel, the big picture. Are the characters consistent? Does the plot hold up? Does it speak to story? Is it boring?! Is it consistent?

How to write yourself a letter for this first big edit: don't worry about the small stuff. Think about big-picture editing. Tell yourself what is working, what you love, remind yourself why you set out to tell this story in the first place. Give yourself that pep talk about what you need to keep doing. Start with what's working.

Then write down what needs to be better. Group this into character, story, plot, setting, tone and pace to start with. Then anything else. This allows you to approach the edit non-sequentially if you'd rather focus on a few bits of character.

4. Now go through the printed manuscript and mark up specific places to work up.

5. Do yourself a quick bunch of sentences about the big moments in the story. Just so you know what is happening throughout.

   Okay. Now you are ready.
6. Open document. Begin edit.

Writing Prompt
(30 minutes)

Because you're about to do a big edit, which feels like a huge task, have a fun-filled, obstacle-filled, consequence-free bit of writing to help you mirror how you might be feeling. You are at the bottom of dragon mountain. Write your journey to the top. Give yourself a minimum of four obstacles along the way, and work out how you will overcome them. Write for thirty minutes.

How do I sequence my story?

We're going to divide your story into sequences, in order to check how structurally robust it is. Now, the action of your story may not follow these sequences. They're more for the character's journey, their arc, their narrative trajectory. So in order for us to check that the plot – the what happens – holds up to scrutiny, we need to check in on our character. Open a Word document, or get eight sheets of paper/index cards. You will write on each card/sheet of paper how your novel hits these story points. Divide it into what is happening for your character emotionally and what is happening externally. Look at the story beats I got you to write before. Now let's flesh them out. Doing this before you do any character work in your editing will help you.

1: Establish the flow of your character's life and what is holding them back. What is the dysfunction they have not grown beyond? Be clear: are they the type of character who a) knows there's more to life than this; b) knows they could/ should change but is resistant to the idea; or c) is oblivious to the fact that change is even possible. Once you know which one they are, what is the external event, the 'life has other plans' event that is going to attack the flow of their life? Be clear to show what your protagonist's life would have looked like if life hadn't had other plans.

2: Destabilized, your character is going to put things right, whatever that means for them. And because these are characters rooted in some universal truth, they'll try to take the easy way out, and put things right, without thought. And because they assume life will return to normal, life still has other plans, and it's going to cause an even bigger predicament for them. This is where the main tension in your story lies.

3: Solve the problem! Choose the easiest solution! But easy solutions snowball! Build the tension. How does this go wrong? How does the character get dragged even further away from their starting point?

4: Things have escalated! Your protagonist is desperate. They're reactive to the destabilizing force in their life. However, they will reach a moment in this sequence where they go from reactive to proactive. Your character will have a reversal of fortune that will hint at a resolution to their story. But they'll see that the way forward is tricky.

5: Now they're being proactive, and actively seeking resolution (rather than reacting to life destabilizing them), they'll move forward. Here, new elements in the story are introduced: new characters, new setting, new opportunities.

6: Your character desperately wants a resolution. And they're approaching having exhausted every single option for them. The only one that remains is the hard one. The one they don't want to do. Here, you drive them to a low point, where they have a glimpse of a resolution, except it's a resolution they do not want under any circumstances. This is where they have to put into action everything they've learned, and find that thing that was within them the whole time, and go for the hardest option. You can only self-actualize if you're utilizing your new knowledge and your untapped potential to do the hardest thing possible.

7: But choosing the hardest option results in unintended consequences. Here, the story turns upside down. But your character has self-actualized. Now they can confirm all their learning and overcome all their obstacles. Often, here we're moving quickly and the stakes are big . . . BIIIIIG.

8: Phew, glad that's all over! We marry the low-point resolution and the mid-point resolution and resolve the tension and all breathe. It's all over.

Your story may not match with the above. But the above is a typical protagonist's journey. You can still subvert this, subvert time, expectation, character and do what you want, but bear the above in mind. You can play with when we meet and leave our main character. You can show us as much or as little of the above. But think of your character's journey in a linear fashion, and consider it in relation to the above before mucking up the order.

Now what you need to do is marry the story and the plot of your book to the above journey. Once you have that down, as you go through your edit, you'll know where all the big story beats are and you can concentrate on making them breathe.

How can I not be boring?

You have to earn your reader's trust. They need to want to spend the duration of a story with you. It is a privilege to get a reader to finish your whole story. Even if it wasn't for them, they still gave you time. And with thousands of novels coming out every year, they were spoilt for choice. They chose you.

So don't bore them, my friend.

Read your work out aloud. You don't have to read the whole thing. But enough to hear the rhythm of it. Once you have the rhythm, you can look at the words, the sentences. Cut out all the adverbs. They slow the pace. The rhythm should be setting any pace. The tone should be setting any mood. The choice of verb should be setting the level of intensity. Too many adverbs and your reader might think, this person is pushing me to read this a certain way.

Sure, a long sentence can be a thing of beauty. But long sentences have to be precise. Read your long sentences aloud. Do you get lost in them? Could a long sentence be three or four sentences? Why does it need to be long? Other than you saying to yourself, 'Wowee, I am quite something when it comes to the ol' long sentence', what is its purpose?

Readers appreciate white space on a page. Don't have blocks

and blocks of text page after page. Break it up. Paragraphs. Dialogue. Give your readers space to catch up with you. Also, pages of italics hurt people's eyes. If I see a page-long paragraph in italics, I will skip it.

Does every sentence count? Does every sentence drive us somewhere? Does every sentence push forward? Does every sentence move forward either character or story or plot or setting? If I deleted this sentence, what would be missing? You're doing a line edit. It's important that you fight for every sentence. This is a long process. Stories aren't easy to write. They take a long time. Editing is precious and drawn out. But it's super important that you, the writer, fight for every sentence and you, the editor, push back on every sentence.

Don't be passive. Don't let your characters be passive. Passive characters are boring characters. If you want to engage your readers, engage your characters. Are they engaged? When they reflect, does this have meaning? A character who only lets things happen to them is one we won't want to sit with for the length of your manuscript.

Consistency is key. Why are you switching narrative voice from third person to first person over halfway through? Why? Know the answer. If the answer is, for stylistic reasons, then ask yourself what the characters need. Show off within the consistency of the novel. Narrative perspective changes are jarring enough when it's multiple voices. When its multiple lenses are hard to keep up with, it makes the reader ask why.

The reader should never ask why you are doing something the way you're doing it. The reader should be engaged and swept away. The moment they ask why is the moment they might let go of your hand. They've lost confidence in you. They'll go their own way now, thanks.

The best bit of editing advice I can give you? If you were the reader, what would you love to read? What would you hate? You are a reader, too. You are an audience member. Use what you love as a reader in how you write.

The other best bit of editing advice? Take your time. Do multiple rounds. You don't need to find a literary agent five minutes after you finish editing. Take your time. A novel is forever. Once it's published, it's done. It's finished. It belongs to readers, not to you. Imagine if you didn't give it your absolute best shot? It might not get published. And if it did, you might know in your heart of hearts there was still work to be done. A novel is forever. So take your time.

Writing Prompt: Edit, Edit, Edit

No one knows what you are writing better than you. Not me. Not your friends. Not any creative writing teacher. None of us knows what you want to do and how you want to do it. Only you know that. Have confidence in what you're doing. All I've done is ask you to ask questions of yourself and consider different perspectives. But I couldn't write the novel or short story or essay you want to write. Only you can. You got this. You can do it. It's going to be hard. You will find yourself second-guessing it at times. But you know the story you want to tell and you know the characters you want to tell the story and you know the setting you want it to occupy. So write, and edit, and edit some more, and take your time. You'll get there.

What makes a great sentence?

A story is a series of sentences, one after the other, that communicate the interior and exterior of a character, their actions, choices, interactions, conflicts and resolutions, in a world that reflects their self-image. A story is also a cry in the dark, a call for connection, a rebel yell, a method of conveying someone's soul. There are practical uses for sentences and spiritual ones. There are sentences that reconstitute the way we look at things. Sentences that are experimental, or seemingly simple, or contain subtext in the space between each word.

How then to advise you on how to write a sentence? Most creative writing tips point to a variance of sentences. A mixture of long ones and short ones. A heady smorgasbord of staccato, abrupt, short, consonant-heavy sentences, heavy with action. And longer ones, that take you on a journey, never letting you take a breath, giving you the world, ensuring you cannot be certain where you'll end up. Creative writing tips also instruct you to think about the rhythm.

But what does any of that even mean? What is the 'rhythm' of a sentence? Of course, this is where punctuation and emphasis play a strong role. A comma can issue a slight pause for a rolling sentence, it can change the trajectory of an action. A specific and active verb can say more than a simple verb with many qualifying adjectives. A simple verb with many qualifying adjectives can sound better, more immersive, more on its feet than a specific and active verb. It could be the difference between 'he sauntered to the kitchen' and 'he walked slowly, relaxed, without a care in the world, into the kitchen'. Much of your choice of sentence depends on the tone of the novel. It also depends on what's happening around it. A sentence, stripped of context, can seem imperfect. A sentence must be precise, even ones that feign looseness.

We need to return to voice, here. Just for a moment, because a sentence may contain the voice of the character, the voice of the narrator, and the authorial voice. In some instances, these are one voice, bound by being the same person, separated, perhaps by time or perspective. The sentence should sound like something the characters would say. But also, it should speak to your own voice.

I couldn't tell you much about my own style that would be helpful. But I know that I want sentences to be characterful and emotional and hit you with a joke, before you let your emotions creep in. This allows me to build an ending that is cathartic and filled with tears. But don't worry, I'll pull you in with the biggest joke I can. There lies my rhythm. In terms of the actual sentences, I like repetition. Repetition of sentence formation, lists, catchphrases, conceits, tropes. Each one, true to the story that it's in, allows me to do the bit of sentence structure you can't teach: make it like music.

Here's what I would like you to do. Find something to record your speaking voice with, be it a smartphone, a computer or a Dictaphone. Whatever is easiest. Think of a story that you tell, be it a remembering from your childhood or that weird and wild thing that happened to you on a bus or on that unexpected night out. Or how you both met. Or how you overcame something. Start recording. Tell me the story. Tell it like there is an audience and you are trying to elicit a certain emotion. Are you trying to make them laugh, cry, think, change their mind, be shocked, scared? What is the purpose of the story? Talk as long as you need. Embellish it if need be.

Now I want you to transcribe it. Do not edit as you go. Just transcribe it. As spoken.

When done, I want you to read it out aloud. Hear the rhythm, hear where it builds and falls. Hear where you speed up and hear where you slow down. Try to understand why you speed up and slow down. Now spend some time refining what you've transcribed, edit it, make it readable. Rather than a transcription of some speech, find the right words. Now read this version out aloud.

Can you hear the rhythm of your recording still? Does it still feel alive or has it flattened somehow? If it has flattened, try to unpick where you've gone wrong. If it feels alive, then great. What do you notice about your voice? Your style? Remember what your intent was with this story, the emotion you were trying to elicit.

Now think about each sentence. Read it out loud. See if you can hear a rhythm to it. Build the rhythm by moving to the next word. Interrogate each word. What colour is the sofa? How quickly did they move? What exactly did his lips do?

I can't help you to write a brilliant sentence. All I'll say is, focus on your voice, what it is and how it is most effectively deployed, and build your sentence up from this. Only you can write sentences the way you write them.

Now let's think about sentences themselves. While I can't help you write a great one, I can tell you some things to think about.

1. Have you chosen your words precisely? Did she sprint or did she burst into a fast run? While both convey the same sort of thing, is one a more precise vision than the other?

2. Is your sentence the right length? Does it outstay its welcome? Is it concise? Is it too short? What information does it convey? Why do we need that information? When read out aloud, is it pleasing? Is it punctuated? Can we read the words you chose to omit? Is the sentence light on its feet, breezy, or is it laden with subtext?

3. Does your sentence make sense? Have you tried to break it, visualize it and put it back together?

4. What flourishes do you use? Is this sentence brimming with adverbs and adjectives? Is there a simile or a metaphor? Does the simile or the metaphor make sense? See point 3 on this list. Have you broken the simile or the metaphor? Have you put it back together?

5. Does this sentence flow into the next one? Does it connect the future sentences to the one that came before it? Is this an inevitable sentence, even if surprising? Is this a superfluous sentence?

6. Does your sentence contain movement? Or is it static? Is it describing something that warrants our time?

7. Is your sentence complex? Plain? Turn a nuanced idea into something accessible? Complicate simple things? Or does it simplify complicated things? Is it what Orwell described as a 'sword of truth'?

8. Where is the logical and where is the lyrical in the sentence? There is the sentence that tells us a functional thing about the story and there is a sentence that sings to you a feeling, an emotion, a wordless cosmic thing of beauty, and there is the sentence that attempts to strike a balance between the two, no?

9. Is your sentence open to the world? Does it invite us in or does it shut us out? Does your sentence make us *feel* something?

10. Is your sentence a lonely commuter, on their way to work, considering another life, projecting their frustrations on those around them, drinking a lukewarm black coffee in a disposable cup, holding onto the pole in the middle of the train car, because if they let go, they don't know where they would land?

How to get feedback

Getting feedback on your work can be tricky. You spend a long time alone with something and you give it to someone else for their take on it, and the feedback comes in and they've either misread what you wrote, given you notes on the book you didn't want to write, made suggestions that don't fit with your vision, torn it apart and made you feel terrible or, worse, said, 'It's great, mate, you're going to sell that in no time.'

All of these types of feedback can be useful in their own unique way. So much of it is preparing yourself for receiving feedback, and being clear on what you want, what is useful to you and what isn't.

Receiving feedback, be it from a trusted writer friend, an organization like The Literary Consultancy, a writing group, your creative writing class or a writing mentor, can be exposing.

Before getting yourself ready to receive feedback, there are some things to consider and prepare yourself for.

1. Remember your intentions. Write down what you want the story to be, to do, to communicate. Write down why you're

telling it, why you're telling it now and what's sacred about it. Keep those close to you.

2. Work out what help you need. Is there something particular you want to focus on? Is it dialogue or story? Or is it a more general read? Do you have specific questions or caveats? If so, I'd wonder whether it's ready to send out. Especially if you know what you need to do. What do you want the person reading this to do and think and feel when done?

3. How do you want the feedback delivered? Do you want it told to you? Over a stiff drink or extravagant ice cream? Do you want the notes in writing? Do you want to see something to digest first before talking through with the person feeding back? Do you want a line-by-line edit or general comments at this point?

4. What questions do you want to ask the person giving feedback? Your intentions will have thrown up a series of things you want and need the book to be. How can you ensure that the feedback you're after covers all these things? This feedback is for you, so make sure you conduct it in a way that feels useful to what you need the most. Otherwise, you might get bogged down in smaller issues and miss a critical conversation about something bigger.

5. Don't be precious. At this point, the book isn't finished. Asking for help and feedback isn't your opportunity to get defensive about how 'it's meant to be this way' and 'I want this character to be unlikeable' and 'the time jumps, I'm sorry you found them jarring but actually there is a symbolic reason for them that speaks to the theme of dissociative depression'. This is time for you to hear what an objective reader thinks.

Readers will project all manner of things on to your book. Their own lives, the book they wish you'd written, the book they wish they'd written, their own political theories, their own take on similar events. I've had one-star reviews from people because my book didn't teach them enough about the British Empire, because the humour wasn't their sort of thing and they don't like funny books, because they bought the audiobook instead of the e-book. Hopefully, this is enough of a range to show you that you cannot control how someone will react to your book. So preparing yourself to receive feedback and being prepared for that feedback can be difficult.

So why get feedback?

What's the point?

Because, honestly, you're too close to the text. You wrote it, you're invested in it, you've lived with it and that means you can't always see what needs to be done. An outsider perspective can give you the lift you need to take the text to exactly where it needs to go.

Now, the problem is, the feedback is going to hurt. It's going to make you feel like starting again, like giving up, like throwing the thing in the bin. It might make you feel like attacking the person giving feedback, telling them they're wrong, they don't know what they're talking about, what the heck do they know, they're not your real dad. You may feel like leaving, changing the subject, crying. You may even feel like they're doing this to hurt you, make you doubt yourself, throw you off course. Are they jealous? Are they literally trying to make you give up? Why do they hate you?

You may feel like they're being competitive, like they think they could do better, like they think you haven't got a hope in hell of getting this published, like they need to be the one to tell you to give up or start again or don't even bother, eat your ice cream and think about retraining as something else.

All of this. Absolutely all of this.

I have felt all of this. With friends, with family members, with people I'm in a relationship with, with my editor, with my literary agent, with copyeditors, with readers.

I'm going to tell you a story that doesn't paint me in the best light in order to illustrate this. I warn you: I do not come over well in this. And that's okay. I own my terrible behaviour.

But it'll prepare you for receiving feedback by seeing how not to receive it.

When I received the editorial notes for one of my novels from my editor, they were thorough, thoughtful and . . . well, there was a lot to do. A lot, a lot, a lot. And the editor wanted me to be prepared to work through them. I had no choice. I had to address the notes. Now, the first thing you need to do when you receive notes is sit with them. Because your immediate feeling will be, no, it's meant to be like that, no I did it that way because . . . And actually, what's happening is, the slippage between brain and page has resulted in something not perfectly executed. And that execution is what needs addressing. Good editors will offer routes forward and trust you to either take that route forward or figure out a new way. Less good editors will say something doesn't work and not articulate why. A good editor is someone you are in conversation with. They are there to help you make the book better. Their thoughts will be invested in getting the best out of you, and they know that you know the book best, so actually, giving you something to bounce off so you can figure out the right way to move forward is a positive step.

I wish I'd kept all this in mind when I received the notes for this particular novel. Because it was an ambitious book, one I had spent many years working on, I found myself defensive about a lot of the notes. I knew they were right, but I didn't want them to be. Because if they were right, maybe I wasn't as good as I thought. A good editor will 'yes and . . .' you a lot, like you're doing improv. This is great, yes to this, and . . . ? Dig deeper. Push it, push yourself.

I was a ticking time bomb of anxiety and stress about these notes. A ticking time bomb needs to go off. And it can either implode, and you internalize all that anxiety and stress and it can paralyze you. Or it can explode and you can . . . well, be a complete idiot, like I was.

I came to a particular note that I reacted badly to. It was about one of the theological elements of the book, and, in effect, my cultural background. It was a tricky note to work through and my editor tried to clarify what I was trying to say, as it was muddled, and they used Harry Potter to illustrate their explanation. I lost my temper. How dare this white person explain my culture to me? It was a real 'I can cuss my mum you cannot cuss my mum' moment. I was furious. And I decided to get my revenge on the poor editor. I copied their comment in its entirety and extended the scene it related to. I had my character find a super specific sub-Reddit that only absolute nerds would know about . . . like the nerds that nerds like myself call nerds. That kind of board. And I created a relay about the theme of the book and I pasted their comment in as a post and I had the other posters tear it apart and humiliate them. I edited the rest of the book, worked hard, feeling lighter, like 'I got one on that person', never once considering that this is an immature way to handle a problem. I submitted the book and felt great.

My editor called me a week later.

'This edit is great,' they told me. 'But I was hurt you did this to me. And used my actual words. I know I'm white and I'm being respectful and open to getting this wrong and being told so, but also I don't know everything and I was trying my best. The best you owed me was a conversation. The worst was to weaponize my own words against me.'

I felt awful.

They continued. 'A good editorial relationship is one of trust and interrogation. You have to trust me to interrogate what you put on the page for me and I have to trust you to take my interrogation in good faith, and if you feel like there's a problem, tell me. We're adults.'

I tried to pass the whole thing off as a joke gone bad. But I knew the truth. I felt like such an imposter, such a terrible writer in this edit, that I had tried to wound my editor in the way they had wounded me: with our words as the weapon.

I apologized. I apologize, still to this day, whenever my editor and I speak. They laugh about it now. And actually, following on from this moment, we had a blissful relationship, and they managed to get the best writing out of me. Because now, we trusted each other. There was probably a less dickish way of getting to that point. But I value the trust I put in them. And we're both proud of the book we put together.

The lesson I want you to take from my defensive cruelty to my editor is: the best way to receive feedback is to know that the person giving it isn't trying to ruin the book or you. They're trying to help you. They will sometimes give you bad advice, the wrong direction, or misread what you've done. You are in control of the book. You have to put the hours in to edit it. They've taken time to give you feedback. Receive it in the spirit you asked for it. Make notes. Listen. Don't react. Don't defend. Just make a note. Ask for clarifications where necessary. Take the conversation (crucially, with the above story: my editor asked if I wanted to talk through the notes and I declined, saying I'd rather get on with it). Sit with their notes. Reflect on them. Work out what is useful and what isn't. Group the feedback into categories: this isn't useful as it's not relevant to this book; this cements what I already feel needs working on; this is working; this is new feedback on stuff I hadn't considered; this is small editorial stuff for once I've done the big stuff.

And then get to work.

How do I write The Other?

While you're editing, it's a good time to think about how you have considered the people in your story whose lived experience is different from your own. There's a case to be made that none of our lived experience is the same and telling stories is a way of me communicating my lived experience to you in the hope that it may tell you something about yours. In this instance, what I mean by lived experience is writing people from different cultures to you, with different worldviews. Men writing women into their stories. White people writing Brown people into their stories. Middle-class people writing working-class people into their stories. Heterosexual people writing queer people into their stories. How do we even consider putting these people, be they ones we have conjured or ones we know, onto the page and ensure we give them humanity, don't reduce them to harmful stereotypes, get stuff wrong about their community and lived experience, or fundamentally misunderstand them?

While you're editing, it is time to consider this. Because the last thing you want your story to do is harm. Right?

Alexander Chee, on being asked how to write The Other, asks the writers to instead ask themselves three questions:

1. Why do you want to write from this character's point of view?
2. Do you currently read other writers from this character's community?
3. Why do you want to tell this story?

I think they're an interesting set of reflective intention-setting questions. So often the question of 'should I write outside of my own experience?' is put on the marginalized. And actually, it's your decision. And if you're going to do it, and make that decision, ultimately owning it, ask yourself these three questions.

There is a lot of nervousness, rightly so, about writing about people who are from different cultures, different backgrounds to you. And I say 'rightly so' because we should treat people and how we characterize them with care. I'm not saying you shouldn't write about people different to you. Oh no, that would be boring.

If writers only wrote what they knew, we would have a monocultural, unadventurous set of books to read. Write what you don't know. But in the same way that you might write a book about a nuclear physicist and thus research nuclear physics, do the same honour to people from different backgrounds to you.

One of the biggest myths about the industry is that you shouldn't write outside your lived experience. I disagree with this. Sure, there are high-profile examples of authors who have got it wrong, edited by editors who didn't realize they'd got it wrong, publicized by publicists who leant into what they got wrong and bought by people who heard all the deafening hype. And the result has been justified critique on social media. I don't think this is any reason not to write outside your lived experience. We are in, as I mentioned before, the imagination business, after all.

All that could be fixed with a simple thing: don't get it wrong.

Write what you don't know. But as you write it, get to know it.

Your job, as a writer, is to be curious about the world, explore the parts of it that you are ignorant of, learn about them and present them back to readers. The best writers are not the ones who suffocate you with their knowledge, but the ones who ask questions and learn the answers, the ones who interrogate their own perception of the world, the ones who start in the dark and move towards the light.

There are organizations set up by ex-policemen where you can hire their services to advise on your procedural crime story. They will talk you through the minutiae of what it is to be a police officer, how an investigation forms, the realities of police life, the toll, the humour and, most specifically, the structure and organization of it. If you're writing a procedural set in the world of the police, you'd better know your stuff. Now, not all police officers are the same and no case goes the same way. But there is a level of authenticity in building the character that needs to be attained. As I said before, you need to confidently lead your reader through the sentences so they don't stop and go, hold on a second, this doesn't work for me.

I'm not saying there's a rent-an-ethnic organization where you can get advice on how to write a Gujarati or a Nigerian-heritage, British-born character or a working-class Bangladeshi from Bradford. Nor should there be. People are different. Their ethnicity isn't an archetype. The way they act isn't stereotypical. These are people. One person's experience isn't representative of everyone's.

The difference with the police officer is, there are certain things police officers have to do when investigating certain cases, certain laws they have to abide by, certain reports to file, certain rules of engagement for interrogation, and so on. There are routines and habits, but also procedures and legal processes they have to abide by.

Writing The Other is about thinking about your power in putting humanity on the page. To add to Alexander's excellent questions, are you perpetuating stereotypes? Are you making this character ethnic in name only? Have you considered the specificity of their life? What brought them to this heist? This date?

Before we even venture towards getting people from backgrounds other than yours to read your manuscript, check that it doesn't perpetuate stereotypes. Lazy writing is reaching for shortcuts. Bad writing is not questioning why you've made someone a certain way without looking at your choice. Offensive writing is when you do all of this, knowing it's wrong.

Perpetuating stereotypes is harmful to communities. It can also mean that some readers internalize the stereotype, others perpetuate and more push against it. It's your duty of care to be on the page confidently. To know that what you're writing presents a person. Now, a person can be flawed and a person can be a certain way that is prevalent in their community and a person can do bad things. But for that flaw to be assumed rather than something within in his character is wrong.

Just take care, is all I would say.

Do your research, speak to people, get people to read your work, don't assume that one person's co-sign is enough for you to think everything's fine. Stress-test it. Read writers from the communities you're writing about. Interrogate your gaze, the lens you cast, the unconscious bias you may not even know you have. Do it well. Take care, and do it well. We're in the imagination business, after all. So don't feel like you can't write The Other. Just make sure you do it well. We've got centuries of shitty stereotypes to break past.

And as an aside, are all the characters in your story from a single background? Why is that? Is there a reason for it? If there is, great. Just an interesting question to ask yourself sometimes.

My final word on this, to sum up this section, is this: you can write about people who come from a background different from yours. All that is asked is that you do it well. You do the work. You do the research. And you understand, ethically, the power you hold in writing about marginalized communities. If you get something wrong, you listen to the criticism and make a commitment to yourself to do better. So do it and do it well. That's all that's asked.

How do I make you laugh?

Sometimes we can be so focused on telling our story we forget to think about how we're telling it. We spoke earlier about the balance of light and shade. Here, while you edit, maybe you can consider whether you can lean into some humour. Writing comedy is about bypassing our brains to deliver either ideas, pathos or good old-fashioned, guilt-free laughs. It's about delivering something so unexpected, out of the ordinary and ridiculous that the reader can't believe their eyes. Sometimes it's about saying the wrong thing at the right time, or the right thing at the wrong time, or instead of saying anything, you crumble and push them over, or saying the right thing at the right time to the wrong person. Mistaken identities, unmanaged expectations, unachievable ambitions, goals achieved that aren't what you expected: these are all the things that make us laugh and laugh and laugh.

If you're writing a comedy book, then go and read Robin Ince's excellent *I'm a Joke and So Are You.*

However, for everyone else, stories need a balance of tone. I don't love reading things that are unrelentingly bleak, or things that are joke joke joke joke, no let-up another joke and when you think an emotional truth might be arrived at, another joke. I want light and shade, balance, good and bad things, joyful times and sad times. And also, sometimes the best emotional jokes can be delivered through comedy.

The natural instinct is to assume that comedy is about people having exaggerated reactions to things. And that doesn't always come up in our real lives, and if it does, it's quite hard to capture without the reader thinking, 'this reads like you reaaaaally had to be there'. Comedy isn't about exaggeration. Often, the easiest way to find a joke is to think, what do people take seriously that shouldn't be taken seriously? The best example of this is the mockumentary *This Is Spinal Tap*. It's funny because the band is good, the lyrics are absurd and the sets are bizarre, and the band members all have uniquely strange ways of looking at the world. But more important than that, they don't realize they're in a comedy film. They take the business of touring a world-class heavy metal band around America seriously. They consider themselves artists. And that's why they're funny. It's why sitcom characters treat their mundane jobs with the intensity of a special crimes unit detective, or people who don't realize their job is inherently ridiculous because they are so single-minded about it. This is a characteristic we can easily apply to those around us.

Another thing is to notice incongruousness and absurdity in serious situations. There's a brilliant bit in the second episode of *I May Destroy You* where Arabella goes with her friend Kwame to report her sexual assault. As they sit there and she answers questions as best as she can, feeling vulnerable, she notices that her friend is playing Pokémon GO on his smartphone. It's a funny moment of humanity, a telling way of showing what people are actually like, and also, how sometimes we might need to distract ourselves at sad times. Michaela Coel referenced that scene in interviews, saying that it really happened. When she went to report her sexual assault, her friend was playing a game on their smartphone next to her. That specificity of absurdity, it can cut tension, show humans for all our complexities and also give subtle character notes about people.

Comedy is ultimately about status. People who are low status wanting to be high status. The power differences between people can be funny. What people do to change their status can be funny. How people acknowledge or refuse to acknowledge their status can be funny. Think of Mrs Bucket in *Keeping Up Appearances*. She is low status pretending to be high status and her pretence and how the reality of her family crashes into her dreams of elitism is part of the running joke throughout. Social status can depict someone's rank in the social order of the world you describe with the leaders at the top and rebels and outcasts at the bottom. The interplay between them can be mined for jokes. Friendship groups, family dynamic, professional workplaces all have these social orders and you should make it your job to interrogate these spaces, work out the dynamics, use them to pull out characteristics and play them for the occasional laugh.

Time plus tragedy equals comedy, goes the famous edict. Partly, this is about distancing yourself from horrific events until you can see the funny side, the absurd ways you and other people may have acted, how a thing that happened at a sad time – a burp during a eulogy, a trip during an argument – that kind of thing. These can enhance the text. Because if it's all one tone, misery, drama, conflict, arguments, sadness, it can be hard for the reader to stay with it. Once you've run the events of your memoir through the sieve of time, what's left? And can you look at it now and see a side you might not have appreciated in the moment?

Writing Prompt: Find the Funny
(1 hour)

Write down a memory that makes you laugh. Think about status within it, where the tragedy is, and what people are taking seriously that they shouldn't. Try to rewrite it so it would make the person who wasn't there laugh. Strip away all the stuff that is irrelevant to the telling of the funny. Push the dialogue, with emphasis, punctuation and tone to make it sparkle.

What should I do next?

It's hard to know when something is finished. I like to think of it as, rather than 'finished', more 'I can't do anything else to this to make it better. I'm moving commas about.' That's usually a sign that you've done all the work you want to do on it. There's the old adage where a story is never finished, only abandoned.

So what to do next? This isn't a 'how to get published' book. There are hundreds and hundreds of those out there. And to be honest, this book isn't about getting published. It's about feeling empowered to tell the story you've always wanted to, and get it to a standard where you want to do something with it.

Here are some suggestions for what to do next.

1. Put it in the drawer. Taking time away from a story can give you an idea of what may still need to be done with it, as well as what you want to do next with it.
2. Find a writing crew to workshop it with. If you want proper robust feedback on your work, research local writing groups or online communities you can join and respectfully critique each other's work. This may help you decide what you want this story to be and what you don't want it to be. Remember the tips I gave you in the section on feedback.

3. You want to write something else, something more. No arguments here. We've only started our journey. Keep going.
4. You may want to find a publisher for this story, be it a place that publishes poems, essays, short stories, articles, life writing or a bigger book-length thing.

The important thing is to not put pressure on what you do next. For me, the work is more important than what I do with it. I like to think of my work as me working through something. I'm not an expert in anything. I am curious. And writing is my curiosity manifesting itself. So for me, a book, an essay, a short story – a story – is all about me figuring something out. What I do next with it depends on the line of enquiry and how it's done. For everything I've published, there is something I haven't that sits happily in a folder on a hard drive, where I gave myself space to work through something. I don't need to publish everything I write, because I'm not writing to be published.

So now you've edited your story, I want you to feel proud you got to this point. Well done!

Take some time off now. You deserve it.

PART 6:

YOUR STORY MATTERS

We are coming to the end of our time together and I want to take a few pages to talk about the work, about you, and about all the other writing advice there is in the world. And then I'll let you go about your day.

We've established that your story matters. If there is one thing I've told you, it's this: if you feel compelled to tell this story, it deserves to be told. As I said in the early bit of the book, there is no recipe for a bestselling story. But there are techniques you can use to empower you to tell the story well. And that's what we've done together. So before we finish up, let's walk through what we've done so far.

1. Your story matters.
2. Learning the technical side of writing is essential, but it should never ever trump your instincts.
3. You know the story you wish to tell better than anyone, but you must also know why you want to tell it, why you're the best person to tell it and why you need to tell it now.
4. Right now, the only person who matters is you, and you, the reader, are the person that you, the writer, needs to do justice to.
5. Writing is incredibly hard.

6. This book, like every other creative writing book, is one way of doing it. You have to find your own way, your own voice, your own path as a writer.
7. If you don't tell this story, will anyone else? If the answer is 'no one', how does that make you feel?
8. To you, your story matters, and right now, this is all that you need to know. The rest will come later.

And let's remember the intentions we set before we started:

1. Why this?
2. Why me?
3. Why now?
4. Who for?

If we've addressed the above, I'm happy. You happy? I hope so. Right, let's move to a final note on craft, a final note on you and then, please give me some time to debunk some writing myths without resorting to snark.

A note on craft

Matthew Salesses writes in his excellent creative writing book, *Craft in the Real World*, that

> Craft is the history of which kind of stories have typically held power—and for whom—so it also is the history of which stories have typically been omitted. That we have certain expectations for what a story is or should include means we also have certain expectations for what a story isn't or shouldn't include.

It is true that so much of our rules around creative writing and how it is taught in this country are based around a set of assumptions: what is the default, what is the other of that default, whose gaze pervades the story and what is of importance in the story. Because I am an author raised in the Western tradition of storytelling, mostly because my reading for a large part of my life was *Marvel* comic books and crime novels, the rules I base a lot of my thoughts on are around the Western narrative of 'the changing man'. A story must exist because a character finds the comfort of their world no longer fit for purpose and goes off in search of something else, or the universe chooses to make a man more aspirational than he is, and forces him to go off in search of a better life, or a man is led into a new world and discovers it either makes him appreciate what he had or it makes him appreciate what his life could be. I purposefully use 'he' a lot here.

It's Vonnegut's 'Man in Hole' again. Into trouble, out of it, better off.

I haven't even delved into other forms of storytelling, other crafts, other techniques, other lenses. Mostly because there are experts out there who know them better. Check out Matthew Salesses's craft book, research things like the keshotenketsu novel and think about what we hold as important in different types of storytelling. Western storytelling can frown on things like coincidence and deus ex machina. Everything must stem, as consequences, from a character's set of choices and how they conflict with the choices of those around them. Which is a heightened version of life. A novel is a set of sequences we choose to show. The interstitial scenes, which a creative writing tutor or a workshop team might highlight as 'wallpaper' – that's often the stuff of life. A novel is what we choose to believe about the actions of a set of characters. A story is a set of choices. However, life doesn't unfold in this way. And if you read enough books in translation, you quickly realize, this is a specific type of storyline that heralds the main protagonist or protagonists as masters of their own universe-in-waiting, and only their actions can get them to where they want to be.

I'm reading about rasa, which is an Indian artistic aesthetic, creating certain feelings in our audience. We will draw them into another parallel reality, full of wonder and bliss, where he experiences the essence of his own consciousness, and reflects on spiritual and moral questions. Rasa has eight separate themes, each one forming a sequence in a story, and each of those themes has a tonal aesthetic and colour palette.

The eight rasa themes are:

Śṛṅgāraḥ: Romance, love, attractiveness. Colour: light green
Hāsyam: Laughter, mirth, comedy. Colour: white
Raudram: Fury. Colour: red
Kāruṇyam: Compassion, mercy. Colour: grey
Bībhatsam: Disgust, aversion. Colour: blue
Bhayānakam: Horror, terror. Colour: black
Veeram: Heroism. Colour: saffron
Adbhutam: Wonder, amazement. Colour: yellow

While I believe that what I present is an accessible version of the mechanics of storytelling, the building blocks of what we deem to be the essence of narrative, there are other modes, and if what I highlight doesn't fit what you wish to do, then please do go and seek out others.

Craft is the way we tell our stories, and yes, there are conventions, but there are no rules. None of these I've set out are rules because they can all be broken. When you're breaking these rules, be bold about how you do it. Be confident. Be you. Be the embodiment of your voice. As we said before, the best stories give as much space to your instinct as they do to conventions, techniques and pre-existing structures. Study craft, but also, don't rely on what has worked before. Think about what works for the story you want to tell.

A final note on you

Your story matters.

That is the crux of this book. The writing is the hard bit, the editing is the harder bit, the finding people to give you the feedback you need is the even harder bit, the getting it to a literary agent is the even hardest bit. And then it's out of your hands until it's ready for you to edit. And then when it comes out, you move on to the next thing because it no longer belongs to you and it's in the hands of the readers now.

Now, people will tell you that it's hard, that they only publish the best stories (which is in itself subjective), that not everyone should be a writer, that not everyone deserves publication. And you're going to listen to these people and nod and smile vacantly, because ultimately that doesn't matter. What matters is that you told this story for you. You told this story because you had to make it happen. My friend Josie Long often says, sometimes if you want something beautiful to exist you have to make it for yourself. And that is the power of storytelling. Our compulsion to tell stories might be that we deem it important for the world, it might be that it will give us a sense of closure on events in our own life, it might be that it's exactly the thing we wish to watch or read and it hasn't been made yet, it may be our way of interrogating society, ourselves, the world, the universe, humanity, the cosmos.

Whatever your reason for writing is, don't feel like there is no space for you to tell your stories. The expectation is that you work hard and tell it as well as you can, and if you're not able to do one of those MAs or courses, then the internet is filled with resources and a thriving writing community exists on various social media sites, and there are podcasts filled with generous writing advice, and libraries can source you a set of great resources. I'll list some of my favourite creative writing books at the end.

All that matters is that you show up. And you do the work. And you write. And you get the story down as you want it to be. And you take time away from it. And you come back. And you read it through. And you think carefully about what it needs. And you sit down. And you show up again. And again. And again. And again. Until you can do nothing else to it. Stories are never finished; they're only ever abandoned. Abandon your story at the point at which you are communicating to the best of your abilities, your ideas and your world to your reader. Remember that the reader brings all of themselves to their reading, and so will project whatever is relevant to them on to the text. So you have to bring all of yourself to the writing.

Trust your instinct. Trust your idea. Trust that if it is important to you, the writer, that your story is worth telling, then it is important to you, the reader, to read it. Trust that if it's important to you, the reader, that this story exists, then it's important to you, the writer, to write it, finish it, abandon it and honour it.

Trust yourself. You know your story best. Only you can write it with only your take on the world. Only you.

Good luck. I believe in you.

AFTERWORD
Ten bad writing tips debunked

I read a lot of writing advice, and I hear a lot of writing advice repeated in my classes and I sometimes despair for writers. Poor people, having to endure so much advice. There are so many books, blogs, podcasts, tips, infographics about writing out there, and some of them are informative, others are inspirational. A lot are weird people projecting their feelings on what your writing should be onto you.

So before we finish up and you go write your story, I'm going to myth-bust some bad advice.

1. **You need to write something that sells:** No, you don't. You write the story you need to write. It has to come from a place within you that needs this thing to come out. Don't put other people's expectations on it. Certainly not when it starts. We can't guarantee what sells; publishing moves too slowly for there to be easy trends and also, if your goal is to be published rather than to write that story you need to write, this may not have been the book for you. Sorry you had to find out in the last few pages!

2. **You need to write 1,000 words a day every day and they need to be perfect if you want this story to**

work: There is no set writing routine. You know how you work best. You know when you write best. You know when you are most inspired. You are not necessarily on a deadline. So take your time, give the manuscript time. Don't try to get it perfect first time; you'll paralyze yourself. Trust in the editing process. Think of weekly targets instead of daily, in order to mitigate the busy mid-week or the low period you might be going through or a day when you're smashing it. Forty-five minutes a day of concentrating is better than writing 1,000 words a day. Some days you'll pad out the word count with nonsense, and when you come to edit it down the line, you'll be mad at yourself.

3. **Rejection means you suck:** I'm not saying this to scare you, but you will receive rejections. I still get rejected from stuff. And I've learned that it's okay. Rejection is part of the process. It's a part of every writer's life. We will all be rejected. We will continue to be rejected even after success. It is part of it. Rejection isn't always about you. Often it's because you sent it to the wrong person. Or you sent it before it was ready. Or you sent it at the wrong time. It's important to know all these things because none of these things is about you. One is about researching the right person to send things to. One is about doing the work to edit. One is about not sending in your novel the week before a huge trade fair or on Christmas Day. Rejection is part of it. What you want in rejection is a helpful one. One that might give you an insight into what you can do differently. Some notes on the manuscript. Maybe that can give you pause to think about whether it's ready. Maybe there is some insight into who might be better suited for the manuscript. Ask nicely. Don't be

mean or defensive. Rejection is part of it. Embrace it and use it to get better.

4. **Your first draft should be with pen and paper:** LOL. Get it written. Don't romanticize how it's written. Find what works for you.

5. **There's a sure-fire way to write a bestseller:** If there was, there wouldn't be so many books, blogs, infographics and courses on how to write a bestseller. There is no formula.

6. **You can't teach someone to write:** This is partly true. But that's mostly because writing is about instinct, inspiration and motivation mostly. It's also about writing. Sure, the technical stuff I've given you can enhance what is already in you. But remember the repeated mantra: your story matters. Also, I can't teach you. I can empower you and share knowledge with you, but the only way you'll get better is by reading lots and writing lots and writing lots in your voice and trying other voices. Sure, sometimes doing this in a supported environment like a course or a writing group can make all the difference, but only you can improve yourself. And you do that by showing up, day after day. Keep showing up.

7. **Writers from marginalized backgrounds should only write about why they are marginalized:** This is nonsense. Write what you want. Anyone who tells you otherwise is telling on themselves. Some people might want to write about race or misogyny or class, others might want to write a banging sci-fi epic. Do what you want.

8. **Write what you know:** This is the imagination business. Sometimes you need to write what you don't know. The best writers are the curious ones. The ones who go on a

journey. The ones who share their interrogation with you. The ones who don't assume they know everything about the world. The ones who want to learn more. The ones who prioritize their questions about the world over their opinions. We're in the imagination business, so by definition you'll be writing what you don't know. And writing what you know is sometimes also being honest about not knowing and the journey to finding out being what you're sharing with your reader.

9. **Show; don't tell:** This is usually overused. 'Show; don't tell' means, don't take shortcuts. Don't tell the reader he's angry; show them through action and dialogue and tone. It's not an edict. Sometimes there is fuel in emphasizing that HE IS ANGRY. Sometimes he needs to say, 'I am angry.' Not everything is subtext. Use 'show; don't tell' sparingly. Don't take shortcuts.

10. **No one cares about your story, so why bother?** You care. And right now, that's all that matters. And I care, I care because I want you to feel like telling your story is worthwhile, for you, for the world, for you, you, you. So if you care, and I care, then you should bother. Say it with me: my story matters.

Now go write it.

Creative writing books to check out

How To Write It: Work With Words by Anthony Anaxagorou
Write It All Down: How To Put Your Life on the Page by Cathy
    Rentzenbrink
*Craft in the Real World: Rethinking Fiction Writing and
    Workshopping* by Matthew Salesses
How to Think When You Write by Robin Etherington
Writing a Novel: Bring Your Ideas to Life the Faber Academy Way
    by Richard Skinner
Elements of Fiction by Walter Mosley
Suppose a Sentence by Brian Dillon
How to Write an Autobiographical Novel: Essays by Alexander
    Chee
The Blind Spot: An Essay on the Novel by Javier Cercas
Feel Free by Zadie Smith
Body Work by Melissa Febos

References

Page xi: Romano, J. (1979) 'James Baldwin Writing and Talking'. *New York Times* [online]. Available at www.nytimes. com/1979/09/23/archives/james-baldwin-writing-and-talking-baldwin-baldwin-authors-query.html [Accessed 19/01/2022].

Introduction: Whose story matters?

Page 6: Smith, Z. (2018). *Feel Free*. London: Hamish Hamilton.

Page 7: Achebe, C. (1958). *Things Fall Apart*. Portsmouth, NH: William Heinemann Ltd.

Page 8: Kureishi, H. (1990). *The Buddha of Suburbia*. London: Faber and Faber.

Page 11: Smith, Z. (2000). *White Teeth*. London: Hamish Hamilton.

Part 1: How do I find my voice?

Page 33: Roy, A. (2004). 'Peace & The New Corporate Liberation Theology'. [Lecture] City of Sydney Peace Prize Lecture. Seymour Centre, Sydney. Available at: www.sydneypeacefoundation.org.au/

wp-content/uploads/2012/02/2004-SPP_-Arundhati-Roy.pdf [Accessed 14/01/2022].

Page 35: Hudson, K. (2015). *Lost Stories, Unheard Voices – Diversity in Literature*. National Centre for Writing [online]. Available at nationalcentreforwriting.org.uk/article/lost-stories-unheard-voices-diversity-in-literature/ [Accessed 09/12/2021].

Part 3: How do I create compelling characters?

Page 113: Salesses, M. (2021). *Craft in the Real World*. New York: Catapult.

Page 133: *Only Fools and Horses*. (1981). [TV programme] BBC One.

Page 140: Vonnegut, K. (2004). 'The Shape of Stories'. [Lecture] University of Chicago. Available at: www.youtube.com/watch?v=GOGru_4z1Vc [Accessed 14/01/2022].

Page 177: Klausner, J. (2014). *Mitch Hurwitz 'Unable to Close Her Eyes'*. [Podcast] How Was Your Week. Available at: howwasyourweek.libsyn.com/mitch-hurwitz-unable-to-close-her-eyes-ep-167 [Accessed 14/01/2022].

Part 4: Setting

Page 208: Abdurraqib, H. (2021). *A Little Devil in America*. London: Allen Lane.

Page 212: Smith, Z. (2012). *NW*. London: Penguin Press.

Page 222: Mantel, H. (2017). 'The Day is for the Living', Reith Lectures. [Lecture] BBC Radio 4. Available at: www.bbc.co.uk/sounds/play/b08tcbrp [Accessed 09/12/2021].

Page 268: Chee, A. (2019). 'How to Unlearn Everything'. *Vulture* [online]. Available at www.vulture.com/2019/10/author-alexander-chee-on-his-advice-to-writers.html [Accessed 09/12/2021].

Page 274: *I May Destroy You*. (2020). [TV programme] BBC Three.

Page 283: Salesses, M. (2021). *Craft in the Real World*. New York: Catapult.

Acknowledgements

No book is written in isolation. No writer is a solitary auteur. Well . . . I'm certainly not. The hard work of so many goes into each book I do. This one, in particular, brings together over a decade's worth of teaching and learning, so I would like to thank as many people as I can that helped me along the way.

Thank you as ever to everyone at my publisher, Bluebird, for making this happen. Thank you to my editor Carole Tonkinson for the vision; to Hockley Raven Spare for the editorial support; to my publicity and marketing people, Jess Duffy, Sian Gardiner and Jodie Mullish. Thank you for the generous (and at times hilarious!) copyediting, Vimbai Shire. Also, thanks, Mel Four, Lindsay Nash, Sarah Badhan, Zainab Dawood, Katie Dent and Holly Martin.

Thank you to Charlotte Atyeo and to my literary agent Julia Kingsford for everything. To my manager Bash Naran, and my agents Nish Panchal, Sam Greenwood and Jason Richman for unwavering support these past few years.

My career only happened because of support from day one from Nii Ayikwei Parkes, Salena Godden, Lesley Naylor, Rukhsana Yasmin, Courttia Newland, Rajeev Balasubramanyam, Deedar Zaman and Niven Govinden. Each of you changed my life in immeasurable ways. I cannot ever pay any of you back. I hope you feel I've paid it forward enough.

Rest in peace to Sam 'State Of Bengal' Zaman and Skorpio the Nemesis, two of my early mentors. Rest in peace to my cousin, my creative partner, my friend, my talented bhai, Steelo Brown aka Styles aka Sanjai Of The Dead aka Buzz LightBrown aka Sanjubhai. Also, thank you to all my English teachers, in particular Mr Roseblade. I still don't feel comfortable calling you Chris.

The close support of the following creatives inspires me to be the best I can be every single day and I would be lost without you: Chimene Suleyman, Josie Long, Nikita Gill, Inua Ellams, Musa Okwonga, Nish Kumar, Vinay Patel, Himesh Patel, Nerm, Anoushka Shankar, Guy Gunaratne, Anthony Anaxagorou and Max Porter.

These writers altered the way I look at reality: Derek Owusu, Yero Timi-Biu, Grace Shutti, Antonia Odunlami, Varaidzo, Caleb Azumah Nelson, Tania James, Kayo Chingonyi, Sabrina Mahfouz, James Smythe, Will Wiles, Tanais, Yashica Dutt, Mira Jacob, Sheena Patel, Sunnah Khan, Roshni Goyate, Sharan Hunjan, Kiran Millwood Hargrave, Saima Mir, Dapo Adeola, Nadia Shireen, Tanya Byrne, Natasha Brown, Teju Cole, Ryan Gattis, Rosie Knight, Nick Marino, Deborah Frances-White, Rachel Long, Bernardine Evaristo, Daljit Nagra, Zaffar Kunial, Leone Ross, Sabeena Akhtar, Huma Qureshi, Lola Olufemi, Alexander Chee, Matthew Salesses, Melissa Febos, Cathy Rentzenbrink, Robin Etherington, Alexandra Heminsley, Angela Saini, Monisha Rajesh, Kavita Puri, Ece Temelkuran, Amrou Al-Kadhi, Furquan Akhtar, Hari Kunzru, Zadie Smith, Reni Eddo-Lodge, Emma Dabiri, Maeve Higgins, Emmy the Great, Mona Chalabi, Nikita Lalwani, Diana Evans, Irenosen Okojie, Suketu Mehta, Neel Patel, Yara Rodrigues Fowler, Darren Chetty, Nimer Rashed, Coco Khan, Fatimah Asghar, Jade Chang, Ore Agbaje-Williams,

Tahmima Anam, Bolu Babalola, Priyanka Matoo, Amy Baxter, Chitra Soundar, Louie Stowell, Mariam Khan, Milli Bhatia, Nirpal Bhogal, Charlie Brinkhurst-Cuff, Liv Little, Season Butler, Candice Carty-Williams, Sharmila Chauhan, Sara Collins, Nandini Das, Juno Dawson, Rachel De-lahay, Laura Dockrill, Hanna Flint, Zahra Ash-Harper, Shruti Ganguly, Sarvat Hasin, Afua Hirsch, Rowan Hisayo Buchanan, Lawrence Hoo, Mahtab Hussain, Theresa Ikoko, Meena Kandasamy, Vanessa Kisuule, Deanna Rodger, Ash Lodhi, Nida Manzoor, Irfan Master, Sarmad Masud, Haleema Mirza, Chigozie Obioma, Ahir Shah, Saima Ferdows, Tejal Rao, Amna Saleem, Pallavi Sharda, Arzu Tahsin, Emma Jane Unsworth, Bisha K. Ali, Mirza Waheed, Caleb Femi, Kerry Hudson, Sunny Singh, Sammy Jones.

Thank you to the editors I've had the privilege to learn from: Gavin James Bower, Rachel Faulkner-Willcocks, Scott Pack, James Roxburgh, Rachael Kerr, Sharmaine Lovegrove, Jean Garnett, Emma Roberts, Carole Tonkinson, Shahesta Shaitly, Katy Guest.

Thank you to the organisations I have taught with over the years, where a lot of these exercises and thoughts crystallized. I hope I remembered everyone: Arvon Foundation, National Centre for Writing, Faber Academy, Spread the Word, *Rife* magazine, Watershed, Bristol Festival of Ideas, University of Bristol, Bath Spa, Word Factory, Rising Arts Agency, Word Factory, Scottish Booktrust, New Writing North, New Writing South, Writing East Midlands, Writing West Midlands, Literature Works, British Council.

Thank you to all my students, all my mentees over the years. Seeing your continued success is reason enough to do any of this.

Thank you to my family. K, S and C, it's all for you as ever.

Also by Nikesh Shukla

Brown Baby

A Memoir of Race, Family and Home

'A beautifully intimate and soul-searching memoir. It speaks to the heart and the mind and bears witness to our turbulent times.'
Bernardine Evaristo, author of *Girl, Woman, Other*

How do you find hope and even joy in a world that is prejudiced, sexist and facing climate crisis? How do you prepare your children for it, but also fill them with all the boundlessness and eccentricity that they deserve and that life has to offer?

A powerful exploration of fatherhood, grief, racism and hope from Nikesh Shukla, award-winning author and editor of the bestselling anthology *The Good Immigrant*.

Available now in paperback, eBook and audio